WINNING

From Backyard
to Greensward
—the Skills,
Strategies and Rules
of America's
Most Sophisticated
Outdoor Sport

CROQUET

Jack Osborn
President, United States Croquet Association

and

Jesse Kornbluth

Foreword by Herbert Bayard Swope, Jr.

Instructional Photographs by William Powers
Illustrations by Alan Scheuch and Willie Espada

SIMON AND SCHUSTER / New York

Copyright © 1983 by Jack Osborn and Jesse Kornbluth

Published by Simon and Schuster
A Division of Simon & Schuster, Inc.
Simon & Schuster Building
Rockefeller Center
1230 Avenue of the Americas
New York, New York 10020

Designed by Stanley S. Drate

Manufactured in the United States of America

1 2 3 4 5 6 7 8 9 10

Library of Congress Cataloging in Publication Data

Osborn, Jack
Winning croquet.

1. Croquet. I. Kornbluth, Jesse. II. Title.
GV931.08   1983   796.35'4   83-677

ISBN 0-671-45824-8 cloth
0-671-47276-3 paper

76.35
0

CONTENTS

FOREWORD

The subtitle of this book might well be "A Story of Reincarnation," for croquet (pronounced now and forevermore "cro-KAY") was buried in the backyards of our country for years. Now it has re-emerged, not only hale and hearty but even in white flannels (where obtainable) on the greenswards of more than a hundred eager clubs from Maine to Hawaii to Alaska.

As this book reveals, the "backyard" or "garden" set game was not the only version of play in America during the past half-century. The first rumble of heavy-mallet, iron-wicket croquet grew to a roar on Long Island in the 1920s, when my father, then executive editor of the late *New York World,* organized weekend games on our lawn in Great Neck. Here, an egocentric and emotional group of non-athletes who mostly comprised the Algonquin Round Table and Thanatopsis Literary and Inside Straight Poker Club—Alexander Woollcott, Dorothy Parker, George and Beatrice Kaufman, *New Yorker* publisher Raoul Fleischmann, Heywood Broun, Marc Connelly, and many others—waged deadly combat.

Although the game was, in those happy, less trying times, played with the same London-made equipment as now, it was not quite croquet as we now know it. The principal difference was the size of the court; at my father's house, croquet balls could be driven with impunity down the sloping drive toward Manhasset Bay. Later, at Sands Point, where Margaret Emerson had a magnificent course, the roots of her trees provided deep snares and impenetrable barriers from which it might take more than one stroke to return one's ball into action.

It was on Mrs. Emerson's lawn that tournament play really began, with Averell Harriman, George Abbott, Howard Dietz, Ogden Phipps and Richard and Dorothy Rodgers, among others, competing every summer until the mid-1950s. Meanwhile, thanks to Darryl Zanuck and Samuel Goldwyn, the game was progressing in parallel manner on the West Coast. Zanuck's challenging but unorthodox course in Palm Springs—there was a fountain in the middle—and Goldwyn's *two* manicured lawns in Beverly Hills saw a whole new group of croquet talents arise—George Sanders, Jean Negulesco, Gig Young, Bill and Howard Hawks, Dick Zanuck, Mike Romanoff and Louis Jourdan.

Although this book touches reverently on that era, its principal emphasis is on the present and the promising future of the sport. The teaching techniques set forth have proven highly effective over the past decade and with study and practice will be of invaluable help to beginner and expert alike.

Although the unlimited playing areas to be found on the courses of the past have shrunk, like the dollar, the game now demands more accuracy than ever. It continues to be chess played on your feet. And the limited boundaries make it more viable for what was once called "the weaker sex."

Skills that once took years to master (mostly by osmosis) are now being acquired in months by neophytes who avail themselves of the competitive joys of club tournaments, which are now played under the same rules across the country.

With the persistence of Jack Osborn, who made the United States Croquet Association come alive, plus the knowledge of the game to be gotten from this definitive book, there seems little doubt that a World Croquet Tournament—with Americans playing a major role—may be in the making before too long.

Herbert Bayard Swope, Jr.
Member, U.S. Croquet
Hall of Fame
Palm Beach, Florida
December 1982

ACKNOWLEDGMENTS

The authors are particularly grateful to William Powers for his crisp photographs, to Cathy Tankoos and Kiley Jones for their assistance with the instructional photographs, Alan Scheuch for his impeccable line-drawings, Willie Espada for his striking graphics, and Mike Hart, Xandra Kayden, Teddy Prentis and Herbert Bayard Swope, Jr., for their editorial contributions. Thanks are also due to Jane Berentson, who, years ago, found a used croquet set at a garage sale, thus effectuating the meeting of the book's junior and senior authors. More recently, Susan Kamil came to lunch, and, after a spirited afternoon of croquet, suggested that the authors meet Dan Green and Bob Bender, who not only agreed to publish this book but have given it a tournament-quality edit. For various other help, the authors owe thanks to Steven Aronson, Jean Arrington, G. Nigel Aspinall, Laura Bradley, Anne Cox Chambers, Jim Daly, Cesare Danova, Barbara Dubisky, Griffin Dunne, Ken Emerson, Richard Illingworth, Katharine Johnson, Richard Kornbluth, Robert Liberman, Tom Lufkin, Eve Metz, Bernard Neal, Libby Newell, William Ormerod, Johnny and Eula Osborn, Kris Palmquist, Amy Robinson, Gerry Sachs, John W. Solomon, the late S. Joseph Tankoos, Alexander Taylor, the croquet associations of England, South Africa, Scotland, New Zealand and Australia, the founders and members of the United States Croquet Association's charter clubs and the members of the current (and future) United States Croquet Hall of Fame.

INTRODUCTION

If this were a word-association test and the examiner suddenly uttered the word "croquet," you'd probably have two responses.

One has to do with a game played in England by the very rich at great country houses. From these houses on languid summer afternoons come the palest of men, effete types who spend their winters dozing over leather-bound books in their libraries. On the lawn, they encounter women who still favor petticoats, long dresses, hats and gloves. Together, they have sport: he taps the ball, then she does. Finally it's time for tea. Oh, what a lovely afternoon! A triumph, in fact. No ungentlemanly displays of temper. No unladylike manifestations of competitive zeal. And, best of all, no perspiration.

The other mental picture is American, and it has nothing to do with gentility. In this vision of croquet, the game is simply a polite form of war. Let's hear no blather about "family entertainment"— this is hand-to-hand combat in suburban backyards. Teeth gritted, sweat escaping every pore, the players stalk one another, trading insults, disputing every shot. What are they waiting for? The moment when they can send their opponent's ball rolling in the general direction of Mongolia. Why are the mallet heads covered with rubber? So the skull of any player who gets bashed won't be mortally wounded. Will they be friends when the game's over? Not if they can avoid it.

It is the aim of this book to banish both of these unfortunate images and replace them with what we know to be the truth about modern croquet: it's the one amateur sport that millions of Americans can play with pleasure all their lives.

Yes, the ultra-chic *do* knock croquet balls around on pristine greenswards at the world's most exclusive watering holes.

And yes, croquet *can* be a vicious game that turns pleasant afternoons into emotional battlefields.

But croquet is much more than a way to achieve status or to vent pent-up hostility. Considered simply as a game, croquet is uniquely satisfying because it never fails to provide the kind of competition that excites, challenges—and enlightens—its devotees. Just when you think you've mastered it, the muse of croquet lands on your shoulder, whispers in your ear, imparts yet another hidden truth about strokes or tactics—and your game makes a quantum stride forward.

Best of all, the pleasure of growing better at croquet isn't limited to any age group or reserved for either sex. One of the better croquet players in America first took mallet in hand when he was ten; now that he's fifteen, he's competing against veterans who were clearing wickets before he was born. And because there's no physical contact and the mallet's relatively light, women can play as well as—or even better than—their male opponents. "You may strain a muscle below the elbow playing croquet," one wit has remarked, "but there's nothing about this game that a drink can't fix."

The pleasures of croquet are not unknown in America: each year, manufacturers say, almost 300,000 croquet sets are sold in this country. Ninety-nine and forty-four one-hundredths percent of those 300,000 sets have short-handled, rubber-tipped mallets, two stakes, small wooden balls and wide-mouthed wickets whose metal uprights are about as sturdy as wire coat-hangers. In the backyards where this equipment is used, it's not unusual for balls to be ricocheted off tree trunks or for the endless paraphernalia of suburban life—swimming pools, driveways, barbecue pits and the like—to be incorporated into the game. With as many as eight players competing on these free-form courts, it's no wonder that matches sometimes seem like European bicycle races: speed contests in which sideswiping opponents is the key to victory.

We know those pleasures. We first encountered croquet in the form of one of those inexpensive backyard sets. We played croquet exclusively with that equipment for years. But these days, when we talk about croquet, we aren't referring to toy mallets, skinny wickets, caroming shots off trees, "take-overs" and arguments that rend friendships. By croquet, we mean "association" croquet.

In association croquet—or as we sometimes say, *real* croquet—the court is more often 84 by 105 feet and clipped as flat as a putting green. The mallets are longer and heavier and are made of specially selected hardwoods. The composition balls are shockingly large—their diameter is only 3/8 inch smaller than the cast-iron wickets they must pass through. There are fewer wickets for those balls to clear, and only one stake for them to hit.

But the differences between 9-wicket backyard croquet and 6-wicket association croquet are as much tactical as they are physical. In association games, players scarcely ever seem to shoot for their next wicket. Their intention, instead, appears defensive—to protect their balls from any possible attack while setting up a controlled offense. As a result, the winner is often a player who's so far behind that he's seemingly out of the game; then hesitation dissolves into brilliantly aggressive shooting, and he suddenly roars out of the backcourt to complete the course and claim the victory.

In 1977, when a small but hopeful group of croquet fanatics founded the United States Croquet Association, very few Americans played association croquet. Considering how expensive it can be to play this variety of the game, it's a miracle that even 100 people made up the five founding clubs—a set of English-made association equipment might cost upwards of $1,200, and the brave soul who decides to create a greensward on his back lawn is looking at a potentially hefty contractor's bill.

If croquet were only a game for the very rich, it would have remained the best-kept secret in amateur sports. But this has not been the case. As of this writing, there are more than 100 clubs affiliated with the USCA—and so many members that the USCA office has had to computerize the national rankings. This 2,000 percent increase in membership since 1977 has made association croquet the third fastest-growing sport in the country.

One reason for our conviction that this growth is but the tip of the iceberg is that American equipment manufacturers have recently introduced sets of association-level mallets, balls and wickets that cost less than $200. At this price, potential purchasers of croquet equipment are thinking twice before plunking down $30 to $85 for a set of toy-backyard equipment. Their considered decision—to buy the Association-approved equipment—is bringing serious croquet to thousands of families who'd never describe themselves as wealthy.

Another reason is that newcomers to association croquet no longer have to create their own greenswards. Country, tennis and sports clubs, capitalizing on their maintenance capabilities, are installing courts, with a few even having taken up the tennis nets on some of their grass courts and introduced croquet wickets onto those lawns. Colleges have added croquet to their sports schedules. And resorts, retirement communities and a score of cities have allocated funds for serious croquet courts.

But the most important reason so many people are playing association croquet these days is even more basic than cost and availability. It is, simply, that association croquet has it all over the backyard game.

The layout of the association game may look funny at first. The equipment may feel uncomfortable. The rules may sound impossibly complicated. And the players—some of them, anyway—may seem not-to-be-believed. If we can only get you to step onto an association court and start to play, however, you'll soon see how little any of that matters. For on the greensward, as afternoon shadows darken the lawn and the faint sound of ice tinkling in frosted pitchers punctuates the steady *thonk* of croquet balls, it will all become clear to you: this is not only a beautiful game, it is terrific fun.

The compelling advantage association croquet has over backyard croquet is that the 6-wicket association game is much more involving. In the 9-wicket backyard game, a highly developed propensity for whacking every ball that ventures near yours is often the factor that decides the match. Association croquet requires much more from you: cunning, patience, courage, skill and a good sense of humor.

Theater critic and Algonquin wit Alexander Woollcott once remarked that serious croquet is "no game for the soft of sinew and gentle of spirit." It is also, as he neglected to add, not a game for the slow-witted or unimaginative. For croquet isn't just a form of war; it's also chess and billiards. And so, along with mastering the technical aspects of the game—how to hold the mallet, and so on— it is essential that you master croquet strategy.

According to movie mogul and croquet fanatic Darryl Zanuck, "You can learn to hit the ball very easily, but to learn the strategy takes a minimum of two years." If, however, you are taught in such a way that you start playing croquet with strategy in mind—if, the first day you take mallet in hand, you can be made to understand that victory consists in making many wickets in one turn, not one in every turn—we believe that you will be playing good strategic croquet within just a few days. By the end of the season, with some practice and guidance, you may well be playing impressive "B"-level USCA croquet. In two years you could be in the finals of the USCA national championships—as happened in 1982 to an Arizonan after less than a year of play—or regularly beating everyone in your zip code.

But can you *really* learn how to play winning croquet from a book?

Historically, the answer is yes. Some of the most brilliant players—many of them women—in turn-of-the-century England learned to play entirely from books, and diligent study of those out-of-print texts would give you a strong sense of the basics. But if you stepped onto a modern greensward and used the strategy you'd learned from those books, you'd have a problem; the game they describe is very different from the game as it's played today in America and in a growing number of other countries.

This book is specifically written for today's players—from beginners to experts. If you've never held a mallet before and have just started to consider the idea of investing a few bob for a backyard croquet set, we feel confident that we will soon have you playing that game with verve and style. If you're presently a backyard player who's wondering why your neighbors are suddenly buying new equipment and arranging their wickets in a different way, we'll show you how to beat them. Even if you are already a member of the USCA and are even now mastering four-ball breaks, take-offs and peels, this book can be a handy reminder of the most basic truths of croquet.

All we ask in return is that none of you drop this book at our feet after you've thoroughly trounced us on the greensward.

1

A BRIEF HISTORY
OF CROQUET

It is said that croquet originated in Southern France in the four-teenth century, when peasants used crude mallets to knock balls through hoops made of bent willow branches. Nonsense. Croquet may well have been invented in the 1300s, but it could never have been played—much less invented—by peasants. The unknown inventor of croquet was, undoubtedly, an individual with a lawn. A man of property. To be blunt about it: someone rich.

Until very recently, croquet was a sport played almost exclusively by the rich and titled. Although you may be tempted to conclude that the reasons were entirely social, they were, in fact, mostly economic. For when you get right down to it, the history of croquet is the history of big backyards.

We don't know who first fenced in the area directly behind the house, thus creating the backyard, but we do know that once European sportsmen began to play croquet on enclosed lawns, they very quickly began to compete at more than the game. In short order, professional groundskeepers were engaged. Lawns became greenswards. And even greenswards were not the last word: in the early 1660s in England, at least one court was made of powdered cockleshells and its wickets were festooned with flowers.

As with all fads, the rage for these early versions of croquet passed, and the game lapsed into obscurity. Then, in 1853, Irish players began to popularize the game. In a matter of just a few years, croquet became a pastime much loved by the English, both for sporting and social reasons. This is hardly surprising: any coed game played outdoors without chaperones would have enjoyed a certain vogue.

Early croquet wickets were as
wide as 18 inches.

But it wasn't just young lovers who took up the game. Sir Walter Peel, who was to become one of croquet's legendary players, first heard about croquet in 1860. In that year, a relative wrote, "We have just had a game introduced here which has taken us all by storm. Eight of us commenced a game after lunch, the interest in which never flags although it lasts until dark, and on one or two occasions we have had to place lamps on the lawn in order to finish it."

With interest in the game growing, it quickly became apparent that no two players agreed on the rules. *Routledge's Handbook of Croquet,* published in 1861, was intended to rectify that, but as anyone who has ever played the game—even with a rule book in hand—knows all too well, croquet players are an astonishingly egocentric bunch, and every last one of them thinks he has devised some improvement of the existing rules. In 1863 such a player was Captain Mayne Reid, an author of children's books, who argued, in *Croquet: A Treatise and Commentary,* that croquet was a character-building alternative to actual warfare—particularly if women could be kept away from the young men who played it. That approach was succeeded in turn by London equipment manufacturer John Jaques, who bought the rights to croquet from a Mrs. Spratt, and, in 1864, printed 25,000 rule books to guide the purchasers of his croquet sets.

Jaques was as happy to sell croquet sets to women as he was to men, and so, in 1866, croquet became a fashionable excuse for England's hostesses to give extravagant lawn parties. At these events, women wore anti-Aeolians—wire cages to hold their skirts in trim during their turns. Despite the skill of some women, they

A Jaques price list from the 1860s.

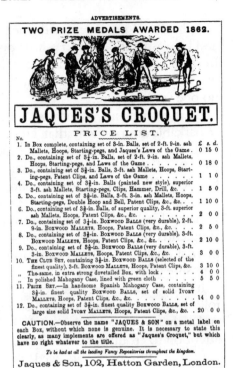

were somewhat patronized by their male opponents, who tended to hold their mallets with only one hand to give the ladies a sporting chance. So heated was the combat, so enjoyable were the parties, that Jaques found himself going back to his printer with an order for 50,000 more rule books the following year.

Eighteen sixty-seven was a landmark year for croquet, not only because almost every English hostess seemed to be sending out invitations with crossed mallets and croquet balls engraved on them, but because, in that year, Walter Jones Whitmore blazed onto the scene.

A young man of considerable breeding but little reliability, Whitmore decided the surest way to create an income for himself was to sponsor England's first croquet tournament. He produced this event at Evesham, on 45-by-60-foot courts that had wickets eight inches wide. To his great good fortune, he won the tournament, thereby giving him legitimate reason to represent himself as England's first croquet champion.

Whitmore had a knack for making enemies, and by 1869 he had alienated both the sporting press and the fledgling croquet establishment, including the All-England Croquet Club he had helped launch. But Whitmore could smell success and money in croquet, and he wasn't about to let a little opposition get in his way. Barred from the AECC, he founded the National Croquet Club. Blacklisted by certain sportswriters, he decided to hold a tournament that no one could ignore.

As it turned out, Whitmore's 1871 extravaganza was the most remarkable tournament that croquet has ever known. Seventeen thousand troops paraded around the courts. There was a full-dress ball. Bands played without pause, and the spectators were packed five deep. Whitmore placed second, but as D. M. C. Prichard writes in his extraordinary *History of Croquet,* it was "croquet as Whitmore visualized it—the pomp and splendour, the extravagance, the dazzling entertainment, the brilliant and aristocratic company and the martial music—and he, Walter Jones Whitmore, at the center, the cynosure of every eye."

It was Whitmore's greatest victory. It was also his last. The following year he was ill, and his tournament had only three players and eight spectators. A year and a half after he made all England pay attention to croquet, he was dead.

Even if Whitmore had lived, the croquet vogue could not have been sustained, for the 1870s marked the introduction of lawn tennis in England—and lawn tennis came on even stronger than croquet had. By 1887 croquet had fallen into such disrepute that the directors of the All-England Croquet and Lawn Tennis Club decided that the placards inscribed with the names of the club's croquet champions should be taken down and thrown into the Thames. Fortunately a groundsman, with a better sense of history than his employers, hid them.

But while croquet was on the decline in England, it was becoming the latest rage in America. Not surprisingly, the rich were the first to take up the game, but clubs and civic groups were quick to follow their lead. Even Rutherford B. Hayes committed $6 of the taxpayers' money for a set of "fancy boxwood balls," an expenditure that enraged the Democratic opposition but allowed the President and his friends to play a higher-quality game on the White House lawn.

Why did croquet sweep a country that had, unlike England, no hierarchical class system? As a Milton Bradley handbook from 1871 suggests, it was because croquet uniquely matched the spirit of a young, aggressive, achievement-minded nation. "When we work or fight, we work and fight harder than any other people," the author noted. "We should be as enthusiastic in our play." The author of the 1865 handbook of the Newport (Rhode Island) Croquet Club saw the attraction of the game in less overtly populist terms: "Whist exercises the memory and the power of calculating probabilities, chess the imagination and the faculty of abstract reasoning, but croquet, though it taxes these mental capacities less, combines them with the delights of out-of-doors exercise and social enjoyment, fresh air and friendship—two things which are of all others most effective for promoting happiness."

For some players, the absence of a uniform set of rules for this new game wasn't a problem. "Croquet seems to have evolved," the anonymous Newport author rhapsodized, "by some process of nature, as a crystal forms or a flower grows—perfect, in accordance with eternal laws." Cooler heads, sensing that a universally agreed-upon code of rules would encourage better play, met on the grounds of the New York Croquet Club at 127th Street and Fifth Avenue in order to form a national association and adopt national rules. On October 4, 1882, that convention, with twenty-five local clubs participating, formed the National American Croquet Association, and the last stumbling block to croquet's ascendancy seemed to have been overcome.

Unfortunately for croquet, bluenoses were discovering that the higher virtues were not all that croquet promoted. As a noncontact lawn sport, it afforded players ample opportunity to consume the dreaded alcohol between turns and for others to gamble on the outcome of the games. And then there was the issue of fine young Christian ladies besporting themselves in the open air; though their costumes and stances seem chaste in the extreme to us now, in the 1880s they apparently encouraged men to think of those ladies in terrible and un-Christian ways. "The game is the gaping jaw of Hades," a right-thinking magazine editorialized in 1898. "It would be well if the enthusiasm of the clergy and laity were enlisted for suppressing the immoral practice of croquet."

Nowhere was the clergy more inclined to do just that than in Boston. Once Boston banned the game, other municipalities began to hide their croquet equipment. At about this time, the rich discovered tennis. Overnight, America's first croquet boom ended.

Just as American interest faded, however, the English rediscovered croquet. In 1896 the United All-England Croquet Association was formed; known now as the Croquet Association, it still rules the game in England. Three years later, the sport, the name—the

Winslow Homer painted this *Croquet Scene* in the 1860s (courtesy, Art Institute of Chicago).

"All England Lawn Tennis and Croquet Club"—and the roster of champions were restored to their rightful prominence at Wimbledon, where they remain to this day.

In the late 1890s a handful of players came upon the scene who were so dazzling in their shooting and in their persons that croquet once again became worthy of widespread public notice.

Of particular importance to croquet's claim to sexual equality was Lily Gower, a tall, blond twenty-one-year-old who'd never seen a tournament and learned all her croquet from books. In 1898 she beat the previous year's winner at Budleigh Salterton. The following year, she won the national women's championship. After two more successive victories in that annual match, she took on a field of England's best male players—and won the gold medal.

Another was Cyril Corbally, who came over from Ireland with Duff Matthews and Leslie O'Callaghan in 1901. These "Irish Terrors" were said to be brilliant shooters and superb tacticians, but nothing about their game was more extraordinary to their English audiences than the way they held their mallets. Unlike every English player in the annals of croquet, Corbally and his friends didn't stroke the ball as if they were playing golf; they faced the ball directly and held the mallet between their legs. In 1902, in his first appearance in England, Corbally won the Open; in the six other championship matches he entered during the next decade, he lost only twice.

Finally, there was Lord Tollemache. Constitutionally irascible, he sought no mentor. Instead, he decided to perfect his game through

INTRODUCTION.

The necessity for a uniform Code of Rules governing Croquet Players throughout the country, has, for a long time been apparent. During the Fall of 1882, players from New York City, Boston, Philadelphia, and Norwich, Ct., joined in a call for a CONVENTION to organize a national association, and adopt national rules. This call was sent to about twenty-five clubs, and on Oct. 4th, 1882, the convention met on the grounds of the New York Croquet Club, 127th Street and 5th Avenue, New York, when the following rules were adopted.

Introduction to the rules adopted at the 1882 croquet convention.

daily practice and sheer determination. Although he never attained the skill of Corbally or Matthews, he did become croquet's premier instructor; as one commentator has written, "Those ready to learn from him on his own terms never had reason to regret it." Happily for us, he published his findings, as *Croquet,* in 1914. This book, with its inspired picture-and-text approach, has helped thousands of English players improve their game.

But celebrated players were not the only reason for croquet's second ascendancy in England. Economics also were a major factor. For the Edwardian era was a time—for the rich and titled, anyway—of country houses with scores of servants, week-long tournaments and no pressing work. Even King Edward fell victim to the croquet craze; when he traveled to Germany for his annual cure, he brought his croquet set along. By the height of croquet's "golden age," there were 170 English croquet clubs, with 120 annual tournaments—not including those held during the winter on the Riviera.

At first, World War I had no effect on the game. On August 4, 1914, there were 9 tournaments. That a war had begun at this time couldn't be determined from the next issue of the *Croquet Gazette;* all the news was of players and matches. By September, however, it was clear that croquet would be suspended for the duration of the war.

In 1919, as England's croquet players regrouped, it became apparent that 20 clubs had been so decimated by the war they couldn't reopen. Although international competition between England and Australia was revived in the mid-1920s, English interest in croquet was on the wane. Fortunately, America once again took up the slack.

The spark of America's croquet renaissance was ignited when Herbert Bayard Swope, the executive editor of the *New York World,* and Alexander Woollcott discovered their mutual passion for the game. As luck would have it, Swope owned a Long Island estate whose greatest asset—in Woollcott's view—was a lawn suitable for a croquet court. It was here that Woollcott introduced dramatist George S. Kaufman and poet Dorothy Parker, as well as others of the Round Table set, to the glories of croquet.

This was not the kind of mild-mannered, highly skilled game the English played but a brand of argumentative, vituperative, highly skilled croquet that Woollcott, more than the others, thrived on. "My doctor forbids me to play unless I win," he announced, and so determined was he to triumph in every match he played that his friends made a film in which he was burned at the stake for kicking his croquet partner. Inevitably, Woollcott and Swope had words over many things and Woollcott retired to his Vermont island and for seven years refused to speak to Swope; Swope was to play more often with Averell Harriman, the diplomat who is remembered more in croquet circles for his exceptional patience and shooting skills than for any of his many accomplishments at the conference table.

On the West Coast, croquet was taken up by movie moguls Darryl Zanuck and Samuel Goldwyn. It is hard to say whose courts were more extraordinary—Zanuck's greensward in Palm Springs had a fountain in the center as an obstacle, but Goldwyn had two tournament-quality lawns on his Beverly Hills estate. Goldwyn had built these courts when he could no longer play golf, and on hot Los Angeles Sunday afternoons, he would often stay away from the games until he had finished his nap. "Then, when we were in the middle of a game, we'd hear the door slam and Sam would be among us," a veteran of those matches recalls. " 'Who's winning?' he'd ask, and then promptly demand to play with the probable winner. He was formidable because he had a shot called 'Sam's crush'—a way of pushing the ball through a wicket. No one complained. It was his court."

Croquet became the weekend passion of Harpo Marx, Louis Jourdan, Mike Romanoff, Jean Negulesco, Howard and Bill

Hawks, Tyrone Power, George Sanders, Gig Young and a myriad of other movie people. Gambling was commonplace—with bets of $10,000 on a single match—but so was "A"-level play. Jourdan, in particular, had a mastery of croquet technique that was equaled only by his splendid self-assurance. Before his opening shot, he would light a cigarette, inhale deeply, and then walk over to the finishing stake. Depositing his lighted cigarette there, he would turn to the starting line and make the first wicket. From here on, he was unstoppable, taking his ball all around the court and back in time to pick up that same cigarette and take one final, satisfying drag before relinquishing his turn.

When Zanuck retired from active competition, Goldwyn's court became the only West Coast greensward of note. Then Goldwyn became ill, his wife turned the water off, and the greensward became, in one player's phrase, "as dry as the Sahara." Diehards produced a sign announcing the Beverly Hills Croquet Club, planted in on Water Department property off Sunset Boulevard and played there for a year without incident, but the spirit had gone out of the game. By the mid-1950s, the only people playing croquet were doing so on suburban lawns with rubber-tipped mallets, thin

Herbert Bayard Swope, Jr. (left), and his father, the executive editor of the *New York World*, discuss croquet strategy on Margaret Emerson's court in the thirties.

W. Averell Harriman sets up on Margaret Emerson's court in Great Neck, a favorite of *The New Yorker* crowd during the 1930s.

wickets, two stakes, and undersized croquet balls, using rules that would have made any self-respecting croquet player consider emigrating to England.

But in the early 1960s, croquet caught on in a serious way with a group of weekenders in the Hamptons, on Long Island. By 1967 thirty gentlemen comprising a cross section of croquet enthusiasts whose home or business found them frequently in Manhattan met to found the New York Croquet Club.

Represented among these gentlemen were the leading players from Long Island, Connecticut, New Jersey's shore, Palm Beach and the West Coast, including veterans of the Hollywood wars. Playing the 9-wicket, 2-stake game, they set up a court in a rambling bumpy glade on the east side of Central Park. By 1969 there were eighty players, and they had begun to experiment with blending the 6-wicket court setting and the basic American rules. In January of that year, the NYCC accepted the challenge of S. Joseph Tankoos, chairman of the fledgling Palm Beach Croquet Club, and the first 6-wicket interclub tournament was held at his Colony Hotel poolside lawn. For historical accuracy, however, it should be noted that some of the matches were held on Mrs. Ogden (Lil) Phipps's rolling 9-wicket lawn and that the finals were postponed for a day so that the competitors could get down to Miami to see Joe Namath and the New York Jets upset the Balitmore Colts in the Super Bowl. This interruption provided the New Yorkers with something to celebrate, for they went on to lose to Palm Beach the next day.

Over the next few years, teams from the Westhamptom Mallet

Beatrice (Mrs. George S.) Kaufman (left) and Harpo Marx (right) watch
Alexander Woollcott take a shot on Woollcott's diabolical court at Lake
Bomoseen, Vermont.

Jean Negulesco lines up a shot on one of Samuel Goldwyn's Beverly Hills courts
as Prince Michael Romanoff and Goldwyn kibbitz.

Club, the Green Gables Croquet Club of Spring Lake, New Jersey, and the Croquet Club of Bermuda entered the fray in both Palm Beach and New York. Once all of these clubs began playing the 6-wicket American rule game, they became the other founding members of the USCA.

With the formation of the United States Croquet Association, in 1977, the game reached a level where it was, at last, poised to make a serious assault on the American sporting scene. Though its aims were ultimately as large as Walter Jones Whitmore's had been a century earlier, the USCA's initial goal was extremely modest—to encourage the formation of enough American clubs to justify a national championship tournament. As Jack Osborn and his associates at the USCA had long hoped, players nationwide came forth, and gathered together in clubs, and multiplied.

Some clubs were tiny: the Chipmunk Hollow Croquet Club of Franklin, New York, consists of one family. Some were imaginatively designed to fit specific needs, such as the Chicago Croquet Club's use of artificial grass in an indoor garage. Others were equally creative: a colorful Texan and his friends started the Aerie Croquet Club on the carpeted twelfth floor of a bank building in Amarillo to avoid the hot summer sun and cold winds of winter and, perhaps, because they feared that if they let the floor lie fallow, they'd eventually divide it into offices and get overly involved in business.

And still other clubs were so wildly improbable that only truly dedicated players would believe in their existence without direct visual observation. Like the Alaska Croquet Club of Anchorage, where the croquet season is the shortest in the world and where most of the year's games take place between 3:30 A.M. and 11:30 P.M. in June. Or the Puget Sound Croquet Club, where Seattle Seahawk owner Ned Skinner has pulled his own end-around play by installing three full-sized courts on his football team's practice field.

With this diverse but impassioned audience for croquet as a base, the USCA quickly found itself growing at a rate that would warm the heart of any corporation president. This growth made the USCA accelerate its plans for the game's gradual expansion, and now it is no longer shocking to hear USCA officials lobbying for national tournament croquet matches dispensed to millions via cable television, croquet as a video game, a USCA–hosted world championship—and even a professional level within the next decade.

In order for any of those dreams to take tangible form, however, it will first be necessary for American croquet players to become more skilled at the 6-wicket association game—the only version of American croquet that can be played as a serious competitive sport. Fortunately, that is no longer a matter of convincing the members of socially exclusive clubs to add croquet to their menu of sports offerings along with tennis and golf. Thanks to the recent introduction of affordable USCA–approved equipment, American players are now able—for the first time—to experience the true game in situations where social status is not a prerequisite.

So all that has to happen for association croquet to become as respectable as its counterpart in England is for the millions of people currently playing backyard croquet with toy equipment to learn that there's another form of the game which is both more enjoyable and more challenging than the one they grew up with. Happily, the introduction of croquet at colleges, the construction of high-quality courts at country clubs and city parks, and the increasing use of association croquet as a backdrop for fashion advertising and BBC television specials have started to make Americans aware of real croquet as they never have been before. It is the authors' hope that this book will help the current croquet movement capitalize on this interest, and that our readers will make this latest chapter of croquet's history the longest and most spectacular of all.

2

BACKYARD CROQUET

by Jesse Kornbluth

In the summer of 1979, I packed up my typewriter, gathered a few books and a lot of paper, and moved my life to Southampton, New York. The idea was to improve my chances of producing a novel about high society as fine as *The Great Gatsby* by spending a summer diligently researching the ways of the old and the new rich. As a member of neither group, I told myself, I had no reason to fear I'd abandon my research in order to become a participant in either old rich or new rich activities.

It is a law of life that resort communities are blissfully sunny from Monday through Friday—and rain-drenched until the weekenders leave on Sunday night. That is how, one wet Saturday morning in June, a friend and I found ourselves at a garage sale examining household artifacts from another era. As rain beat against the garage, we imagined, as best we could, that we were in an attic, hunting for old treasures; in that spirit, we quickly decided to buy a child's blackboard ($2) and a knocked-together Fellini-blue work-table ($5). And then we saw the mallets of an ancient croquet set sticking out of a grocery bag.

This set was $4, so we bought it. We didn't have much of a backyard—a 20-by-30-foot lawn at one side of which grew a tree whose roots bulged like muscles just below the surface of the grass—but a croquet set seemed like something every house in Southampton should have, even if the dwelling in question was a small farmhouse on the fringes of the estate area. Having done our civic duty, we put our mallets, balls, stakes and wickets on the front porch. Then we forgot all about them.

Forty days or so later, when the heavens cleared, we dragged our new toys out back and laid out the court. Or, rather, we improvised, for we measured nothing. Boundaries? We had no need of them; if a ball went under a bush or car or couldn't be hit, a player was to move the ball a mallet's length away from the obstacle. Where to put the wickets? We just stuck them in the ground in a pattern that vaguely resembled the diamond-wicket layout of the game we'd played in our youth. Preparing the lawn? Why, we'd had the grass cut just a week before.

With this devil-may-care attitude, we weren't distressed to learn that our set came with only 8 wickets. Like thousands of backyard-croquet players before us, we improvised a solution: I took pliers in hand and cut a wirehanger to make the 9th wicket.

It goes without saying that we had no rulebook. But in backyard croquet, the absence of a rulebook is no great disadvantage: there are always at least two players who know *exactly* how the game is to be played. As we were sharing this summer house with four other experts, there was never any danger that we would all agree about the rules, and so a great deal of pre-game time was spent discussing

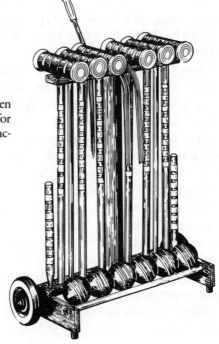

Backyard croquet sets like this have been mainstays of summers in America for generations (courtesy, Forster Manufacturing Company, Wilton, Me.).

such technicalities as take-overs, the penalty, if any, for hitting the ball twice or just pushing the ball along, and the number of shots you have if you hit another player's ball just before or after your ball clears a wicket. These disputes sometimes lasted even longer than our games—but no matter how much we argued with one another, a situation inevitably arose in the first few minutes of the match which had not been covered in the rules conference.

Eventually, we hammered out a set of "house rules" and settled down to play croquet. Or our version of it, anyway. You may recognize some of our most cherished precepts from your own backyard experience. They included:

1) No matter how many players there are in the game, each player shoots with only one ball.

2) If you hit another ball, you get two shots. The first shot can be taken two ways. One way has you setting your ball next to the ball you've hit, planting your foot firmly on your ball, and smashing your opponent far away. The alternative is to place your ball a mallet-head away from the ball you've hit, and shoot your own ball toward the wicket or another ball.

3) Because most of the men who eventually competed on our court had some experience playing in active sports and most of the women were lifelong smokers, women were allowed as many take-over shots as they liked. In particular, women were encouraged to take the opening shot of our backyard game—the shot through the first and second wickets—as many times as they needed to clear both wickets in a single shot, thus giving them two shots to make the third wicket. Men, on the other hand, were allowed no take-overs at any time. Worse, men with demonstrated proficiency at croquet were required to take an unspecified percentage of their shots with their mallets held in one hand.

True to the psychology of croquet players everywhere, my friends and I believed that the rules we played under were, simply, *the* rules. To us, all regulations not used on our lawn were bogus and not to be discussed. Because we were so vociferous—and because it was our lawn, our equipment, and our iced tea—we were able to convince all the people who played with us that the sport we regularly beat them at was croquet.

If any of those people are reading this, my apologies.

For what we were playing was not croquet—it was a form of tag played with mallets and balls. At first we didn't understand this, so great was our enthusiasm for whacking the balls around. But as we got a sense of the rhythm of our game, we began to see that every game was fundamentally alike: one player invariably took an early lead with his single ball, and the rest of us chased after him. Late in the game, when someone was ahead by a large margin, we would band together against him and try to prevent his victory with desperate cross-court smashes. Other than that, our only applications of strategic thinking consisted of a more or less knee-jerk application of the Hobbesian view of life—that every man is at war with every other man.

Despite the predictability of our games, we played croquet so fanatically that all thought of writing *The Great Gatsby* passed from my consciousness, and I commenced to live a modest version of it. The modest farmhouse was now "Airedale," the tiny lawn became "the greensward." It was only a matter of time before my friends and I would decide to sponsor a tournament and call it the "Airedale Invitational."

Acquiring appropriate prizes was no problem; we bought inexpensive "gold," "bronze" and "silver" medals at an athletic-supply store and threaded red, white and blue ribbons through them. Arranging the tournament itself, however, was more of a challenge. One of our more sophisticated players suggested we contact the New York Croquet Club, on the theory that croquet was such an undeveloped sport in America its officers would help even us. Which was exactly what happened: once Jack Osborn finished laughing at the idea of a tournament on a bumpy backyard, he not only gave good advice, he offered to drop in for a few moments.

At the time, I had no idea this was an offer of any significance. Only later would Osborn confess that he long ago pledged to have nothing to do with backyard croquet—the concept of the game, the equipment or the strategy. This is not an inconvenient oath: it enables him now to avert his glance while this backyard-bred writer attempts to make a case for the beauties of the backyard game.

On the afternoon of the Airedale Invitational, though, Osborn showed up like the Johnny Appleseed of croquet. Unlike the rest of us, he wore a white shirt, white shorts and white Tretorn sneakers. He owned his own mallet, a full-sized English thing endorsed by someone named John Solomon. Clearly, if correctly importuned, he was willing to give a demonstration of the sort of croquet we had seen only in English movies.

With Osborn's appearance, both the matches and the arguments ceased, and twenty ordinarily verbal people lined up quietly behind the chalked baseline to watch a master at work. Osborn did not disappoint. He stroked his ball smoothly, controlling his shots even on our joke of a greensward. But he didn't shoot for the wicket; instead, he seemed to want to be sure he hit every other ball on the court before he went through. And having cleared one puny wire hoop, he moved all the other balls around some more, leaving himself an easy shot at the next wicket.

So deft was Osborn's shooting that one of the more knowing among us shouted, "Jump shot! Jump shot!" Osborn looked up and smiled. Then he picked up a ball and set it a foot from the next wicket. "I'm 'dead' on this ball," he announced. "If I hit it with the ball I'm going to shoot, I'll lose my turn." With that, he positioned another ball—the ball he intended to strike—2 feet from the wicket. And then, hitting the ball at an angle that suggested he wanted it to burrow through the Southampton dirt and emerge in China, he got the sphere to fly over the "dead" ball and sail through the wicket. We were, without exception, amazed.

Osborn left soon after, and the Airedale Invitational resumed, but his aura lingered, for a few of us, anyway, and we resolved to upgrade our game. This is a resolution that millions of backyard croquet players have undoubtedly made over the years, but we had one great advantage: we knew how to reach Jack Osborn. For Osborn, zealot that he is, cannot disguise his hope that any player sufficiently curious about the backyard game to want to play it better just might be prodded to take up the association game. As a result, Osborn has—albeit indirectly—given me a number of hints that have made our backyard games much more like the game he loves.

If he has not yet been able to get us playing association croquet, there are reasons. For one thing, when my friends and I want to play croquet, we aren't able to do so on tournament-quality greenswards or even, for that matter, on full-sized 105-by-84-foot lawns. Nor, until the recent introduction of affordable English-style equipment, were we able to use mallets, balls and wickets that were appreciably better than the $4 set that first lured me to croquet. Finally, the only guide we had to backyard croquet was the pamphlet that came with our backyard set; though admirable for its brevity, it offered no suggestions for improving the strategic level of our play.

But with this book and perhaps some upgraded equipment in your possession, you should be able to play a more interesting game of backyard croquet—and play it better—than those of us who have been duffing around backyards for years. If you are now bracing yourself for a long lecture about a complicated game with hundreds of things to remember, relax: there are few apparent differences between the backyard game you may now be playing and the USCA version. What you will soon understand, to what will probably be your great surprise, is how radically those few changes will affect your game.

How many aspects of your current version of backyard croquet would the USCA like to change?

Just three.

In order of importance, they are:

1) You must learn to "take croquet" after you've hit your ball against another. To understand what's called for here, you must forget about your cherished custom of setting your ball a mallet-head away from the ball you've hit—or, as croquet players say, *the roqueted ball*—and then taking two shots. Similarly, you must banish from your mind all thoughts of placing your ball against the roqueted ball, putting your foot on your ball, and whacking away. Instead, as we explain more fully below and on page 49, you must *place your ball against the roqueted ball and take croquet*.

What does this mean? Merely that the first shot of the two shots you've earned for hitting another ball should be—must be—a *two-ball* stroke. You move your ball next to the ball you just hit, and without the help of a controlling foot, you hit your ball and move it and the other ball. Thus, you'll have a dual intention for this shot. First, you want your ball to go to a spot where you can do something useful with it on your second shot—like clearing a wicket or hitting another ball. Second, you want the roqueted ball to go to a spot where you can, in the near future, use it again.

The ability to send those two balls where you'd like on the croquet stroke is the essence of good croquet on both backyard courts and tournament-quality greenswards. As we will tell you time and time again in these pages, making a single wicket is nothing—making them all is *everything*. The way you do this is to move your opponents' balls to places where you can use them again as steppingstones for the rapid completion of the course. In short, you must master the croquet stroke.

To say more about the croquet stroke here would be overly technical and unnecessarily confusing. But after you've finished this chapter and have set up your backyard court, take this book outside with you and turn to "Breaks" on page 130. Once you have grasped the concept of break-making and learned one shot—the split shot, described on page 118—you will have mastered the single most important strategic principle of high-quality croquet. Should you decide, at some later time, to move up to "association" croquet, you'll already be well-practiced in the kind of shot-making that is the hallmark of that game.

2) The kind of backyard contest in which each player uses one ball and as many as six players are on the court at any one time is also to be forgotten. *When you're playing against one opponent, each of you will use two balls; only when you're playing doubles—with four players on the court—are you responsible for a single ball.*

At first, this may be confusing for you. Not because you'll have trouble remembering the correct order of play—that's easy enough—but because of the concept of "deadness." As those who have played croquet before will recall, you're "dead" on a ball after you've struck it with your own. The only way to remove that "deadness" is to send your ball through its next wicket. Otherwise, if your ball hits the "dead" ball again, your turn ends.

When you're playing with only one ball on a court that's littered with balls, it's easy to accumulate "deadness" on as many as five balls—but it's also relatively easy to clear yourself of "deadness" by going through your next wicket on the same turn. With only four balls in play and two balls to think about, however, it's less likely that you'll rid yourself of "deadness" in a single turn—and far less likely that you'll remember which of your balls are "dead" one or two turns down the line. In order to keep disputes about "deadness" from ruining your games, you will either have to build a "deadness board" (see page 62) or keep a pen and notebook with you on the court in order to make a running account of the game.

3) The shafts of backyard mallets are so short that there's not much reason for owners of backyard equipment to study the chapters in this book about grips and stances. And because the balls used in backyard sets are proportional to the rubber-tipped heads of those mallets, you'll have to use them. But you can do something about the wickets, and, if it's at all possible, *you're advised to buy 9 of the white "winter wickets"—or as they're sometimes called, challenge hoops—that are used in association croquet (see page 58) and replace the wider, thinner wickets that came in your backyard set with them.*

Because it's more challenging to shoot for a smaller target, these wickets will reduce the likelihood that a lucky shot will determine the outcome of the game. In an idealized setting—a lawn of putting-green texture, with equipment of the best quality—nature and technology have been so manicured and perfected that luck scarcely plays any part. Obviously, on a bumpy backyard lawn that probably isn't even regulation-sized, you can't hope to control the variables to the degree possible on a greensward. But you can, by substituting association wickets for backyard ones, establish a level of play which rewards the steady shooter who can execute the fundamentals properly. And should you choose to play association croquet at some point in the future, not only will you not be intimidated by the narrowness of association wickets, but you'll have mastered them.

And that's really all you need to change in order to play a better, more authentic game of backyard croquet.

Yes, you could set up your backyard wickets in a 6-wicket, 1-stake configuration so your game is a miniaturized version of true association croquet. But as I've learned the hard way, those who are unfamiliar with that setup may be too intimidated by it to enjoy the game—or you may find yourself coaching your untutored opponents so constantly that your own game suffers. Just as people who have just learned to ride a bike don't immediately jump on a racing bicycle, those who have just developed an affection for backyard croquet don't necessarily want to abandon it for what seems like a slower, more intellectual game. They may eventually come to see that the seemingly slower, seemingly more intellectual 6-wicket association game is, in fact, much faster and livelier than 9-wicket backyard croquet, but in order to reach that point, it's usually necessary for them first to satisfy their appetite for aggressive, shoot-first-and-ask-questions-later play.

If you are one of those players who are attracted to the 9-wicket, 2-stake game because it's a socially acceptable form of warfare, it's entirely possible that you'll never get past this stage. That's fine with us. But I would make one small recommendation to you as you rush out to play the game that's more fun than any book—in addition to reading the few pages about breaks, croquet strokes and deadness boards, which I've urged you to take to heart, turn to page 174 and read the United States Croquet Association's rules for 9-wicket croquet. True, your backyard set probably comes with a pamphlet which seems to tell you—in less than a page—all you'll need to know about the regulations of backyard croquet. In fact, as you'll soon find out, disputes occur over points too obscure to be covered by the rules included in any pamphlet. You need not memorize the official USCA rules, but you should be familiar with them so that, in the heat of play, you can find the relevant rule at a moment's notice and authoritatively—and correctly—cite croquet writ.

Finally, you may discover that a summer-long obsession with backyard croquet leaves you with no desire to pick up a mallet again. Don't blame croquet—blame your equipment. Disenchantment with the backyard game is the first sign that you're ready to move up to association equipment. You may want to use this equipment on a 9-wicket backyard course, or you may want to try your hand on an actual greensward. No matter. The important thing is that backyard croquet, having provided you with a season of fun and good fellowship, has performed its ultimate service; it has led you to discover the very real rewards to be derived from croquet in its most authentic form.

3

ON TO THE GREENSWARD:

An Introduction to American 6-Wicket Croquet

by Jack Osborn

Like those of almost all American croquet players, my roots are deeply embedded in the backyard game. Even now, having played thousands of times on some of the finest association courts in the United Kingdom, South Africa, Australia and America and having delivered my sermon about "real" croquet at uncountable clinics and tournaments, I still have precise and affectionate memories of playing 9-wicket, 2-stake croquet on warm summer afternoons. There I am calculating the best angle to hit an opponent's ball on the Long Island backyard that sloped down to Beaver Dam Creek; here I am smashing my ball over the bumpy grass at the Westhamptom Mallet Club's courts. Rubber-tipped mallets, coat-hanger wickets and spirited debates—yes, I've known those joys.

It was, in fact, because of backyard croquet that I first encountered the man who would serve as the inspirational force for my eventual dedication to the sport of croquet. His name is John Solomon, and when I met him in 1967, he was on his way to amassing 50 international and national titles, a record no other player in the world has come close to matching.

John had come to Westhampton Beach as the captain of a visiting team from London's Hurlingham Club. This team was to compete in the second meeting between the venerable English club and our group of American upstarts. The first match, a year earlier, had been played in England under English rules; this time, the British would be playing 9-wicket, 2-stake croquet on our turf.

It goes without saying that the Westhamptonites had not fared well in England in that first contest. But playing on our 2-inch grass and using our rules and court layout, we felt we'd do much better this time. So confident were we that we might even emerge victorious that we generously provided our visitors with advisers to help them with our rules.

The New York Times headline "Croquet on Long Island Baffles Britons" will give you an idea how well our advisers did. Our players did somewhat better, achieving a 3–3 tie after three days of play in a steady downpour that might well have been imported from England.

It would be pleasant to report that this tie was the result of brilliant shot-making and superb strategic thinking by every American player, this correspondent included. Alas, the truth is more complex. For although we did play decently, our biggest asset in those matches was probably our guests' dependence on their "advisers." Those advisers, being American duffers who were not sophisticated about the intricacies of croquet shot-making, didn't realize how much more advanced the visitors were—and because the advisers couldn't make certain shots, they never suggested them to the British.

After the first day of play, however, Solomon and his gang didn't rely so much on their advisers. Incorporating the niceties of English croquet strategy into our game, they began taking shots none of us had ever seen before. Full rolls, pass rolls, long split drives—these remarkable shots were used to start three- and four-ball breaks. Clearly, this was a level of croquet we Americans had no knowledge of.

The following year, when our team traveled to England for the third match in this evolving international series, the English thoughtfully offered us some advisers. We jumped at the chance to use them: far from disadvantaging us, these players could help us advance our game to our hosts' level.

I arrived in England a full week before the matches were scheduled to begin and went directly to Hurlingham, home of the world headquarters of croquet. There, under the tutelage of my English mentor, the late Ian Bailleau, and John Solomon's lovely mother, I practiced until some of those advanced shots and a few of the British Association's laws began to sink in. By tournament time, I was primed for the event.

Of the thousands of croquet matches I've played over the years,

The Hurlingham Club of London has, since 1959, been the headquarters of the Croquet Association. The courts in the foreground are more than a century old.

there are two whose memory I particularly treasure. That game at Hurlingham was one of them.

That I would lose was a foregone conclusion: my opponent was John Solomon. That I would score what was for me a very impressive 8 points to Solomon's 26 was less predictable. But even more than those 8 wickets, I savored being on the same court as Solomon and watching, firsthand, his masterful display of shooting. For despite my week of practice and my diligent reading of English croquet texts, I had no idea how large an arsenal of shots there was or how precisely a truly skilled player could place a croquet ball.

No American fared better than I did that day, and the final score was 8–0. Far from feeling humiliated by the defeat, I felt exhilarated by the possibilities it suggested. As I left the court, I was determined to learn all I could about the game as Solomon and his teammates were playing it.

In an article he wrote for the British *Croquet Gazette* after these matches, Solomon was as generous as he'd been throughout the contest. "I think only two things are needed for America to become a serious threat to English croquet," he wrote. "One is an English-type lawn; the other is the formation of an American Association for the purposes of reaching agreement between clubs on the rules of their own game as a preliminary to scrapping them altogether in favor of our own."

In the fifteen years since Solomon made those suggestions, there have been great strides toward achieving all but the last. Over the course of a decade, enthusiasts from all across the country met frequently on greenswards and in smoke-filled conference rooms to hammer out the first set of rules for 6-wicket, 1-stake American croquet. As a result of those gatherings, the United States Croquet Association was established, giving American croquet players an association that allows them to compete locally, regionally and nationally under rules they all share. With that encouragement, English-style croquet lawns have sprouted up on American soil; there are now more than 100, with as many more being readied for play.

Of these many accomplishments, none impresses me more than the adoption of a single set of rules. Each of the framers of these rules brought to the debate the certainty that his was the only game to play. Reaching agreement was, therefore, a painful task. On one thing, though, there was surprising unanimity: no one felt we should, as Solomon suggested, scrap American rules in favor of the laws of the British Association.

There were several reasons for this unanimity.

While we conceded that the 6-wicket, 1-stake course was a more challenging test of shot-making, we felt that many of the other British idiosyncrasies couldn't be introduced here without permanently alienating most of the Americans who were the backbone of our young association. We decided, instead, to keep the essence of

John Solomon, the perennial captain of the English national team and, since 1981, the president of the Croquet Association, now holds more than 50 international titles.

the American backyard game and join its fast-paced, "go-for-the-wicket" spirit with the English court layout. The resulting game, we discovered, was not only more fun to play than backyard croquet; it was, we sensed, more fun to watch than the English game.

Interestingly, our English friends have also found that American croquet now has what they'd probably describe as a certain charm. Although they remain wedded to their own conservative game and their own laws, they have played the new American game often enough on our courts to take it home and try it out. In several instances, they have even introduced it as a tournament event on their own courts.

Ideally, of course, croquet players the world over would play the same game according to the same rules. It is hard to imagine what would have to take place in order for that to happen. The British laws remain the closest thing to the world standard, as much by tradition as by strength of numbers. If growth is considered a factor, the American game might predominate. If numbers alone matter, we would all play according to Japanese rules, for two to three million Japanese are now playing a game they call "gateball" with as many as ten players on the court at any one time.

The most important development on the international scene, for the present, is the increasing frequency of international matches. In 1972, as the result of another of John Solomon's suggestions, we invited a young Englishman to come to the United States and give lessons to the members of the New York Croquet Club, the better to prepare them for international competition. G. Nigel Aspinall, then twenty-six years old, had already distinguished himself by beating John Solomon several times; he would go on to win ten President's Cups in England, which is like saying he won the world's singles championship ten times. But more important for American players, he crossed the Atlantic six times during the past decade, each time giving those fortunate enough to learn from him more insights about croquet than they would have acquired in years of unsupervised play.

By 1981, American croquet had advanced to the point where it made sense to establish U.S. Challenge Cup matches between the top American players and their counterparts from other English-speaking countries. The success of these matches was assured when England agreed to send a team to Palm Beach and play half of its games under English laws and half under USCA rules. And what a team England sent! John Solomon, who came out of semiretire-

Nigel Aspinall, currently England's and the world's top-ranked player, jumps his ball over a wicket during one of his frequent visits to Palm Beach.

ment, captained the foursome, with Professor Bernard Neal, Dr. William Ormerod and Nigel Aspinall himself filling out the group.

Against this awesome squad of multi-titled internationals—all of whom had represented their country against Australia and New Zealand in the Macrobertson Shield International competition—the United States fielded three-time U.S. Singles champion J. Archie Peck, two-time doubles champion E. A. (Teddy) Prentis IV, Teddy's father, E. A. (Ned) Prentis III, who was a veteran of the 1968 Hurlingham matches, and this writer.

It would be sweet to report that after fifteen years of instruction from our English friends, we finally had parity with the English team, or, better yet, that we routed them, but neither of these dreams became reality. In spite of our much-improved play, the record book shows the score as England 15, USA 1.

The USCA 1982 International Challenge Cup Team which tied Scotland and lost by one match to South Africa. From left to right, back row: E. A. (Ned) Prentis III, Stan Patmor, Jim Bast, Richard Pearman, Archie Peck. Front row: Kiley Jones, Jack Osborn (captain), E. A. (Ted) Prentis IV.

That one victory? Modesty gives way to pride here. It was my other most memorable match. I beat John Solomon, 26–5.

Aside from the undeniable pleasure this win gave me, I relate it here because it underscores, I think, two of the most attractive aspects of croquet. The first is the fact that *any* player can, with practice and patience, improve his or her game dramatically. Second, and more intriguing, is the fact that on any given day, it's possible for *any* player—even one ranked far below his or her opponent—to win, and win handily.

My victory over John Solomon is hardly the only proof of this phenomenon. Much more impressive is the fact that the 1982 USCA International Challenge Cup Team won fifteen of its thirty-two matches against Scotland (7–7) and South Africa (8–10), with five of those victories attained under unfamiliar English rules. Among these Americans were a fifteen-year-old, some players who took up the game just a few years ago, and a number of malleteers who hail from places that their English, South African and Scottish opponents had never heard of. For American players to come from historically unimportant places and yet be able to compete on some of the world's most revered greenswards is reward enough; to hold our own against classically trained opponents is a welcome bonus. Clearly, our instructional efforts to upgrade the level of American play are starting to pay off.

4
THE OBJECT OF THE GAME

(With a Keynote on Vocabulary)

As we examine the basic points and objectives of the American 6-wicket game, let us stress the importance of learning and understanding the language of croquet. If you are to comprehend what follows, it will be impossible to do so without first distinguishing between such words as "roquet" and "croquet."

Soon enough, we're going to be throwing shorthand phrases around which will depress you no end if you don't understand them. You must, therefore, learn some basic croquet vocabulary even before you begin to play. Fortunately, croquet terminology is accurate and brief.

In this chapter we will italicize key words. If they are not made sufficiently clear by the text, please turn to the back of this book, where there is a glossary of croquet terms. There, we define just about every croquet term you'll ever encounter. Here, we stick to the basics. They are:

roquet—A roquet is made when you hit your ball so that it strikes another ball.

croquet—The *croquet stroke* is the first stroke of the two you earn by roqueting another ball. To take croquet, you place your ball against the roqueted ball and hit your ball so that both balls are moved.

rush—to rush a ball is to roquet it in a particular direction or to a particular spot.

deadness—every ball is said to be "alive" on all other balls at the start of the game. Thereafter, a ball acquires "deadness" by roqueting another ball. It cannot roquet that ball again until it itself has cleared its next wicket; until then, it's said to be "dead" on that other ball. If the ball roquets the "dead" ball again before the next wicket is cleared, the striker's turn ends and both balls are put back where they were.

The object of the American 6-wicket game is to beat your opponent(s) around a course of wickets and hit the finishing stake before he does (they do). The game can be played by either two people (singles) or four people (doubles).

In the singles game, each player plays two balls, either Blue and Black or Red and Yellow, and attempts to score 12 wicket points and one stake point for each of his balls for a winning total of 26 points before his adversary.

In doubles, the game is played between two sides, each side consisting of two players. One team plays the blue and black balls and the other the red and yellow balls. Each player plays the same ball throughout the game. As in singles, the object is for one team to score the total of 26 points before their opponents.

In both games a ball scores a wicket point by passing through the wicket in the order and direction shown in the diagram on page 52. This is known as *running a wicket*. But a ball that has first hit another ball (roqueted) cannot thereafter in the same stroke bounce off and score a point for itself, except at the first wicket. A ball that has scored all twelve *wicket points* is known as a *rover*. The rover can score the stake by hitting it. When time has run out in time-limit tournament games, and neither side has scored the 26 points needed for victory, wicket (and stake) points are added at the end of the time-limit and the team with the most points is the winner.

Play is made by striking a ball with a mallet. The player who is doing this is called the *striker,* and the ball that he strikes, the striker's ball. The striker may never strike an adversary's ball with his mallet. But by striking his ball against any other, the striker may cause that ball to move and/or score a point.

The players play each turn in the sequence blue, red, black and yellow. A player is initially entitled to one stroke in a turn, after which his turn ends unless in that stroke his ball has scored a wicket point or hit another ball. When the wicket is scored, the striker is entitled to play one additional or *continuation stroke*. When another ball (whether opponent's or partner's) is hit, the striker is said to have made a roquet on that ball and is entitled to two extra strokes. He then becomes dead on that ball.

The first of these two strokes is known as the *croquet stroke,* and it is made after the striker moves his ball to and places it in contact with the roqueted ball.

If, in the croquet stroke, the croqueted ball is sent off the court, or the striker's ball is sent off the court without first having made another roquet, the turn ends. During the turn, a striker may roquet each ball he is *alive* on once. He may make a further roquet on each ball provided that his ball has scored a wicket point for itself and has thus *cleared* itself of its deadness. Thus, by a series of strokes that entitle him to continue, the striker may make one or more points during one turn. Such a series is known as a *break*.

But *continuation strokes* are not cumulative—you cannot clear a wicket, hitting another ball in the process, and collect three strokes. If a player first clears a wicket and then, on the same stroke, hits another ball, he may either take one continuation stroke and not be dead on the ball he's hit, or he may choose to roquet that ball and take two strokes. If a player makes a roquet as a consequence of a croquet stroke—if his ball not only moves the ball he's taking croquet on but goes on to hit yet another ball—he immediately takes croquet on that ball and continues to play. But if, during a croquet stroke, a player scores a wicket for his ball, he is entitled to only one continuation stroke, which is his reward for clearing the wicket.

A ball is said to be *out-of-bounds* when its vertical axis rolls more than halfway over the boundary. It is then known as a *ball-in-hand.* This term is also used to describe a ball that has made a roquet, or any ball that must be picked up and moved.

After each stroke, all balls off the court are replaced one mallet head in from the point where they went out. This is also true of all balls within 9 inches of the boundary line after each stroke, except the striker's ball. These balls are replaced a mallet head (9 inches) in from the line.

With these introductory objectives in mind and before we explore any specific tactics or strategies, let's look at the court layout and direction of play along with the equipment you will be using for playing the game.

A Championship set of Jaques croquet equipment.

In Chapter 5 you will find a chart that delineates and correlates the different types of equipment available and its appropriate use by type of lawn, cost and level of play. Those who are planning to buy new equipment will find that this chart can keep them from wasting money on equipment better than they need—or from buying an inexpensive set in the belief that all official-looking equipment is more or less the same.

5

THE COURT AND EQUIPMENT

The Court

If you happen to have a spare lawn tennis court handy, it's a simple matter to convert it to a tournament-quality greensward. If, however, you have somehow misplaced your lawn tennis court, be of good cheer, for you are not alone. Most of today's better American players don't play on their own greenswards and are quite content to perfect their game at United States Croquet Association clubs (see USCA Member Clubs, p. 218). Should you aspire to be a Class "A" tournament-level player and can't recreate the tournament lawn, you should, in any event, try to play on a 105-by-84-foot tournament-sized court. (Such courts can be divided into two courts for beginners and intermediate players and for practice sessions.)

Others make do with lawns that were never intended for use as croquet courts but have, with a bit of rolling and reseeding, proved perfectly adequate (see The Lust for Lawns, p. 165). Obviously, if your home is set on a lot smaller than one acre, there's almost no way you can create a quarter-acre rectangle for a tournament-sized court. Still, if you have a clear, level lawn that's 50 by 40 feet or larger, you have enough room for a proportionally correct, scaled-down court. Simply take care to maintain the 5-by-4 ratio or as close to it as possible.

Ideally, you will have four colored flags to mark the corners (blue in #1, red #2, black #3 and yellow #4), but whether you do or not, you should indicate the out-of-bounds line with one-sixteenth-

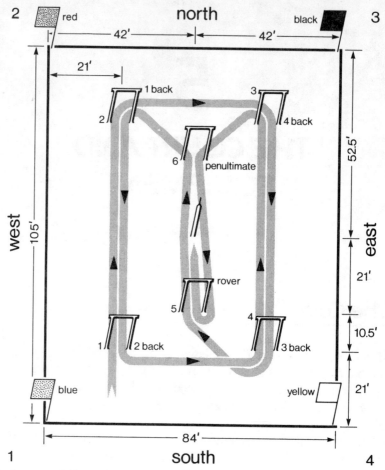

The layout and direction of play on the official United States Croquet Association 6-wicket court.

inch string stretched at ground-level from corner to corner, affixed by a golf tee or metal pin at the corners. If you have a set of flags for the corners, they are *not* to be used in lieu of the golf tee or metal pin, as you may need to remove the flags for shots from the corners. Nor are lime or chalk recommended for boundary lines; even at their sharpest, they don't provide the definitive boundary line that croquet requires.

As diagram 1 indicates, each corner of the court is assigned a number. For purposes of description, the boundaries are designated North, South, East and West—regardless of the actual geographic layout of the court. The wickets are also numbered. With the exception of four wickets in the 9-wicket game, each wicket has two numbers, one referring to its order in the outward-bound direction, the other to its position in the homeward-bound direction.

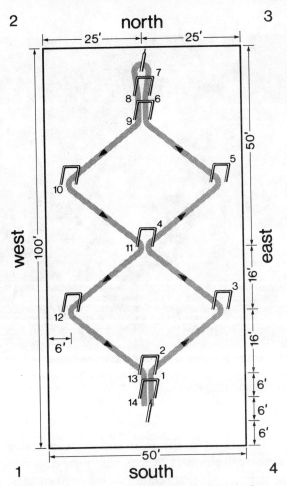

The layout and direction of play on the official United States Croquet Association 9-wicket court.

If you have a 100-by-50-foot lawn and are playing 9-wicket croquet according to the official United States Croquet Association rules, you will set your two pegs 25 feet from each sideline and 6 feet from the north and south boundaries. Wickets 1 and 2, as well as 6 and 7, are set 6 feet apart, with 1 and 7 set 6 feet from their respective pegs. The corner wickets (3, 5, 10 and 12) are set 34 feet from the North and South boundaries with their centers 6 feet from the sidelines. The 4th, or center, wicket is set 50 feet from the North and South boundaries and aligned with wickets 1, 2, 6 and 7. The 9-wicket court can also be scaled down, but not smaller than 30 by 60 feet.

The 6-wicket, 1-stake game is simpler to lay out. (Don't be fooled; this is the only way it's simpler than 9-wicket croquet.) The peg is set at midcourt—52½ feet from the North and South

Corner flags and boundary lines: Boundary-line string should not be tied to corner flag since a flag may need to be removed during a match. Use a golf tee or metal pin pushed completely into the ground.

boundaries; 42 feet from the East and West sidelines. The four corner wickets are positioned 21 feet from their respective North or South boundaries, with their centers 21 feet from their respective East or West sidelines. The two inner wickets are set 21 feet from the peg, with their centers 42 feet from the East and West sidelines. The inner wicket nearest the South boundary is known as the rover hoop. It is the last wicket to be made before completing the circuit, and, for that reason, is painted red across the top. The first wicket has a crown painted blue.

At the risk of repeating ourselves, we urge you yet again to spend a few minutes memorizing the order of play. Once you're out on the greensward, you won't be able to consult this book between shots, and you can be sure that your opponent will maintain perfect silence as you send your ball through a wicket that's not on the approved order of play. At that point—and only then—will he remark that your turn is over and that no additional shots are due you. If he is particularly disagreeable, he will cite not only the correct order of play but this paragraph as well. We would hate to see our text thus used, so—*memorize the order of wicket play!*

Equipment

THE MALLET

"The croquet mallet," writes an English authority, with characteristic English understatement, "is a long-handled hammer." A 2½- to 4-pound hammer, to be precise, with a round, square or rectangular head that's made from a 9-inch-long, 3-inch-wide block of such exotic hardwoods as lignum vitae, teak, boxwood, rockwood or mahogany. The shaft is generally about 36 inches long and is made of ash, hickory or malacca cane. At the top of the shaft is the octagonal grip. Almost inevitably, some kind of string, leather or cork has been wrapped around this end for surer handling.

The mallet is the one piece of croquet equipment that can be personalized. As a result, once a fledgling croquet buff feels the onset of an addiction to croquet, he often can become obsessed with his mallet in much the same way as a runner can be preoccupied with a particular brand of running shoes. Does a square-headed mallet with brass fittings on the head perform better than a round-headed mallet? Does a player who holds his mallet in a way popularized by some great Irish players do better with a mallet whose shaft is 4 inches shorter than the standard English mallet? Does it make sense to buy any mallet not made by John Jaques &

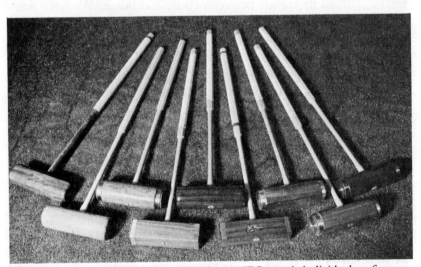

Mallets: A variety of mallets from "A" class to "D" to suit individual preferences based on weight, shape, shaft style, handle trim, binding (brass or nonbound), quality of wood and price (all by John Jaques & Son).

Son, Ltd., the English firm that has been manufacturing croquet equipment since 1850 and currently finds itself swamped with orders for mallets costing as much as $200?

Whatever mallet you choose, there are a few simple rules that, if diligently followed, will enable you to make a mallet a once-in-a-lifetime purchase.

1) When it is not in use, never leave a mallet leaning against a wall; this will warp the shaft. Instead, hang it upside down between two pegs in a cool, dry place.

2) After a match on wet grass—and given the fact that a croquet match is almost always played on days when it just happens to rain, it would be more accurate to say: "After *every* match"—towel your mallet dry. If you're extra fastidious, you might, from time to time, waterproof your mallet head with a thin coat of shellac.

3) *Never* throw your mallet in anger at another player or, even worse for the mallet, at a tree or building. As tradition dictates, the only direction the mallet is *ever* to be thrown is skyward.

And that's it. For all its apparent delicacy, the mallet is a sturdy tool, and there's no reason to go overboard protecting it. In the 1930s, Harpo Marx air-conditioned a room specifically to keep his mallets properly cool, but no one who played against him ever remarked that his chilled mallets improved his game. Nor will you find it necessary to commission Louis Vuitton to protect your instrument on its travels between court and home. We have heard that idea expressed—by a woman who commutes from Palm Beach to Southampton, with barely a week in New York for shopping purposes—and we find it a bit of overkill.

Hand-sewn mallet cases, however, can be seen on airplanes with greater frequency. If you anticipate that you'll be toting your mallet around the country with you, you'd do well to have one of these cases made. Although an occasional airport security guard will insist that a croquet mallet could be used as a hijack weapon, that is no reason to allow yours to be banished to the hold; if you aren't allowed to carry it aboard, you can usually convince the security guard to store it in the captain's cabin.

Even if you never play croquet and simply buy a class-"A" mallet for its looks, you have, at the very least, become the proud owner of a conversation piece that has charms that, say, a baseball bat can never hope to equal. Some croquet addicts, upon reading this, may think of applying their mallets to our heads just for acknowledging that anyone might flirt with croquet for overtly social reasons. But our view is that it doesn't make any difference how or why people come to croquet, so long as they actually get to the greensward. In our experience the gent who buys a mallet simply to impress his business associates or friends will inevitably find himself taking mallet in hand, improvising a wicket, shooting a few impromptu hoops—and, not long afterward, heading off to the nearest lawn to try his luck at the thing itself.

THE WICKET

For those whose memories of croquet are all about rubber-tipped mallets and thin wire wickets, no encounter with regulation croquet equipment is more disquieting than the first heft of a half-dozen association croquet wickets. Not only do these wickets look heavy, they are heavy: each one is 6 pounds. That's because association croquet wickets are made of cast iron that's 5/8 inch in diameter, because they're 12 inches from crown to ground, and because they have carrot-shaped spikes that thrust 8 inches deep into the turf so there's no possibility that a firmly-stroked ball will unsettle them.

Wickets are also known as hoops, but that word, with its

The 8-inch carrot-like spikes of the Jaques championship wicket hold it steady no matter how hard a ball hits it.

implication of vast diameters, is misleading. Hoops suggest vaulted arches that give balls plenty of room to bounce around before they get through, but association wickets aren't like that at all. These wickets are 3¾ to 4 inches wide—a scant ⅛ to ¼ inch wider than association balls. There is only one exception to this hoop width. The winter wicket—Jaques calls it a "Challenge hoop"—is made of thinner, ⁷⁄₁₆-inch diameter bent steel, giving the shooter slightly more margin for error on courts where the grass may be irregular and the ground may be frozen.

Considering the weight and thickness of these wickets, new owners of association equipment may be inclined to drive them into the lawn with the help of a hammer. Don't! At the very least, a hammer will chip the paint; at the worst, fracture the cast iron crown or upright, or, in the case of the winter wicket, distend the uprights. If you must use a hammer to set your wickets into the ground, put a block of wood across the crown first. If you are an equipment fetishist, there is a wooden hammer called a "smasher" that can be purchased for just this chore.

Players who devote any time at all to the game or whose lawns are frequently used by others will soon discover that croquet balls will, inevitably, create grooves through the center of the wicket. These

Three kinds of wickets and balls: Left, a championship cast-iron Jaques wicket with an Eclipse ball. Center, a Jaques "Challenge hoop" (also known as a winter wicket) with a composition ball. Right, the standard wire wicket used in backyard croquet with a lightweight wooden ball.

grooves give an equal disadvantage to every shooter and may well cause the ball to roll back into the jaws after it has passed through a wicket. This can prove to be costly if the match is a close one, so if grooves form in front of your wickets, you should, between games, rotate them—the important thing is to make sure that the outside wickets retain the correct alignment. To achieve this, simply rotate the wicket so that one of its present holes is used. Be sure to turn your wickets in the same direction so there is a clear, straight shot from one outside wicket to the next.

THE BALL

The key ingredient in evaluating a croquet set is the ball. Compared to the milled wooden or lightweight plastic balls used in backyard croquet, class "A" association balls seem like the giant steel ball-bearings used by shot-putters. Designed in proportion to association wickets, these balls weigh a pound, give or take $1/4$ ounce, and are $3^5/8$ inches (plus or minus $1/32$ inch) in diameter. They're made either of compressed cork covered with high-impact plastic or of a recently developed solid plastic composite. Whatever their center, their surface is usually lightly textured or milled.

Aside from the weight and diameter requirements set forth in both USCA and British Association standards, the ball played in all sanctioned tournaments throughout the world must meet another criterion involving its elasticity.

To meet this critical requirement, a ball must have a rebound coefficient of *between* 27 and 33 inches when freely dropped from 60 inches onto a 2-inch steel plate embedded in concrete. Any bounce greater would be considered too "hot" or lively; any lesser bounce would be insufficient. USCA class "C," "D" and "E" balls usually fall into the high-bounce category, and also vary in weight from 9 to 14 ounces. These livelier balls are often found preferable on heavy lawn as they require less strength to propel long distances.

Since 1938, Jaques has enjoyed a monopoly in the production of its class "A" level Eclipse ball, but recent efforts by the English Sports Council and an American developer hold great promise that a homogeneous composition ball will fulfill all the criteria—including a difficult-to-define proper sound a ball must make when struck—and meet the worldwide standard set by the Eclipse.

An association croquet set comes with four of these balls, solidly colored blue, red, black and yellow. In singles, one player will play red and yellow, the other blue and black. In doubles, each side plays either the red/yellow or blue/black pair.

There is another set of balls especially colored so that two matches may be played on the same court at one time: in England this is called "double banking." To avoid the confusion that similarly colored balls would inevitably create, these balls are colored green (for blue), pink (for red), brown (for black) and white (for yellow).

THE FINISHING STAKE

Those who are planning to play 2-stake, 9-wicket croquet with association equipment better order an extra peg, because a basic association set includes only one. It stands 18 inches tall, and is 1½ inches in diameter; it is made of wood and, like the wickets, has a sharpened point to keep it firmly in place. It also has a narrow wood or plastic spire on its top. This extension serves to hold the clips of the players who are shooting for the peg. (The designer was a believer in close contests: the spire is large enough to hold several clips.)

Although painted white, the peg has four bands of color on it, with blue at the top, then red, black, and yellow. These colors are hardly decorative; rather, they indicate the order of play. Aside from the "deadness board," the peg is the only spot on the court that gives this information, and even expert players will find themselves consulting it when there is no strategic reason to, simply to keep themselves from one of croquet's most egregious and common errors: playing out of turn.

Stake (or peg): Center stake (or winning peg) has black extension for clips on top with colored stripes in sequence from blue, red, black and yellow downward to white base.

Jack Osborn has also decorated all his tournament mallet shafts with tape bands in this color sequence as a personal reminder to avoid this painful fault.

CLIPS

In a game with no scoreboard, blue, black, red and yellow clips are attached to the next wickets that players must clear. A clip thus reminds a player—who may well be executing a series of shots that seem to have nothing to do with clearing wickets—which wicket his ball is for. And for knowing spectators, a survey of the clips indicates where the players are relative to the peg, thus providing what passes in croquet for the score for each ball and side.

On the outward course—the first six wickets—clips are placed on the crown of the wicket you're shooting for. On the homeward route—those same six wickets, cleared in the opposite direction—clips are placed near the top of the wicket's upright. When you're shooting for the peg, clips are placed on the peg's spire.

The only time a clip isn't on a wicket or peg is when you've cleared a wicket and are continuing your turn. Then it's attached to your shirt, belt or trousers pocket. When your turn ends, it's promptly set on the next wicket your ball is for.

Because association croquet is often characterized by defensive tactics so seemingly perverse that players often appear to be avoiding wickets, clips are absolutely essential. Most players *think* they're

Clips: Clips of plastic (or metal) on top indicate which of first six wickets a ball "is for." The homemade (from a hair roller) clip on the side shows that the colored ball "is for" one of the six hoops on the return route.

aware of where they're bound; the clipped hoops, however, *know*. In association croquet matches, the only time a referee may offer advice without its being requested by a player is when he admonishes the shooter to set his clip correctly. Many is the croquet player who has avoided a humiliating error by this advice—or simply by noticing, on his own, where he's ultimately going.

THE DEADNESS BOARD

Even deluxe English croquet sets don't come with deadness boards, which means you're going to find yourself, at some early point in your croquet career, buying wood, hinges, and red, yellow, black and blue paint and making one of your own. Or, if you prefer, you can have someone else purchase these items and build one for you (undoubtedly at inflated prices). You cannot, at the present time, do something so sensible as buy a ready-made deadness board, though at some point in the future, a crafty entrepreneur is going to make a fortune—well, a *small* fortune perhaps—manufacturing this item. For one truth we know: it is very difficult to do without a deadness board.

The function of the deadness board is to serve as a kind of interim scoreboard, telling you what balls you must not hit upon penalty of committing a foul and ending your turn. Let's say you're shooting with the black ball, and having cleared the second wicket, you roquet the yellow ball. A referee, another player, an appointed board-keeper, or, if necessary, a spectator, should promptly turn over the yellow flap that's on the same line as the block of black wood. This indicates to other players—and to your forgetful self— that you are "dead" on yellow until you've cleared yourself by running the next wicket.

Let us say that by dint of clever shooting, you go on to roquet red. Now your red flap is put up and you're two-ball dead. Finally, you roquet blue. The blue flap is opened, and you're three-ball dead. Woe to you if you end your turn without running your next wicket and "clearing" the deadness board, for you will then be in a terrible jam: balls that are not dead on you can dart fearlessly into court-space you formerly controlled and use your ball as a steppingstone without fear of retribution. Darryl Zanuck's description of this state, though harsh, is exact: "When you're three-ball dead, you're just a worthless bum."

To make a deadness board, buy a 36-inch plywood square, four

The deadness board advises players which balls they may not roquet until they clear their next wicket. In this example, blue (at top) is dead on 3 other balls, red has just become 1-ball dead, black is dead on 2 balls and yellow dead on 1.

thin strips of wood as long as the width as the board, four 6-by-4-inch blocks of wood, twelve 4-inch squares of wood and a dozen small hinges. Attach the strips to the board at regular intervals, and paint the board-*cum*-strips glossy white. Paint one of the 6-by-4-inch blocks blue, another red, another black and the last one yellow, and attach them to the deadness board to the left and just above the strips of wood, with blue at the top, followed by black and red, with yellow at the bottom. Paint the face of three of the 4-inch squares of wood with either of these colors and the back of all the squares white and attach the squares with hinges to the top of the wood strips, making sure that you do not put a blue square on the line of the blue block, a black square on the line of the black block, etc.

Other variations on size of these boards are larger (5 by 5 feet) or smaller (1 by 1 foot), depending on your court size and spectator considerations. Other materials such as plastic (colored sink stoppers hung on nails) and metal (painted coffee tin tops on magnets) can also be used.

CLOTHING

One aspect of croquet which traditionally has kept prospective players away from the game is the notion that only certain clothes may be worn—and that the player who ventures onto the croquet lawn in lesser gear will, to his humiliation, be asked to leave. While it is certainly true that croquet attracts its share of snobs, we have never heard of a neophyte who fled the court because he was wearing the wrong shirt. In croquet, as in life, snobbery usually takes more subtle forms.

For purists, there is one outfit that might be described as the regulation croquet uniform. The shirt is white, Sea Island cotton—no polyesters need apply—and the sleeves are rolled to a point just below the elbow. The trousers are white flannel. Pleats at the waistband and a slight flare in the leg are optional; a generous cut to allow freedom of movement is essential. The shoes are white tennis sneakers, the cleaner the better. If a hat must be worn, a trilby is the ideal choice.

It can't be denied that a deeply tanned croquet player decked out in these duds lends a certain class to any greensward he deigns to walk upon. Considering how far this image of croquet players has traveled, it may be more to the point to emphasize how many first-class players wear none of the above.

For croquet players—like all sports fanatics—tend to wear those clothes in which they do well. White is still preferred, in fact, required in USCA major tournaments, but heavy flannels have given way to tennis shorts, long-sleeved shirts to short-sleeved golf types. For the superstitious, it doesn't matter how ratty these clothes may become; if a certain shirt was worn on the first day of a tournament and the player won in it, he may continue to wear that shirt right through the finals. Others won't change their socks. Gone, however, are the days of bizarre combinations like red socks and purple sneakers. Glare has given way to comfort.

Once the requirements of comfort have been met, there are really only two articles of clothing which a player needs in order to feel comfortable on the greensward.

The first is a good pair of sneakers. Spiked heels, cleated golf shoes and any other footwear that might damage the lawn are, obviously, not allowed, so players with a tendency to experiment in their attire occasionally drift away from sneakers to try boat shoes or other momentarily fashionable sport shoes. Try these if you like, but for consistent support, high-quality tennis shoes can't be beat.

The second is an umbrella. In most sports, an umbrella wouldn't be considered clothing, but it is a law of life that it invariably rains on days when croquet matches are scheduled. On those rainy days, you can tell the rookies from the veterans; the veterans carry large golf umbrellas. Because there is no rule that requires players to lend their umbrellas to their opponents, they will often appear to be deaf when a drenched rookie requests the shelter of his opponent's umbrella while he makes his shot. The next time out, he will, almost invariably, be carrying his own umbrella. Privately, he may remark how quickly he is learning the game. And he is, he is.

THE EQUIPMENT CHART

The most enjoyable croquet is played by those who use equipment that is appropriate to their lawns, abilities and aspirations. With the variety of croquet sets now on the market, it may be difficult to figure out which set is best suited for your type of lawn and your level of play. The accompanying chart should help you determine the set that's best for your needs.

The descriptions, weights and estimated costs of the sets and their components that we describe in the first four classes in this chart are based on the standards set by England's leading maker, John Jaques & Son, Ltd. American manufacturers are beginning to develop better-quality sets to meet these standards. To find out where these sets are available in your area, contact the United States Croquet Association, 635 Madison Avenue, New York, New York 10022, or call 212-688-5495.

For the purposes of this chart, all basic sets for USCA and British 6-wicket croquet will consist of the following:

4 mallets
4 balls (blue, red, black and yellow)
6 wickets
1 finishing stake (peg)
1 USCA Rule Book (includes rules for 6-wicket and 9-wicket croquet and golf-croquet)

Those who intend to play 9-wicket, 2-stake backyard croquet should be aware that they will need to buy three additional wickets and one additional stake.

USCA Classification and Price Range	Basic Set Designations	Set Components	Weights
A ($900 to $1,400)	**Championship**	MALLETS: Round/square, Brassbound heads, grips Cane spliced, sight line.	2½–4 lbs.
		BALLS: Eclipse (or equivalent).	1 lb.
	Association	WICKETS: (Association) Cast iron.	6 lbs. each
		1 stake (peg), USCA rules, flags, clips and markers in a wood storage box.	75–77 lbs. per set
B ($600 to $1,000)	**Club** (or Roehampton)	MALLETS: Round, Brassbound, grips, sight line.	2 lbs. 4 oz. to 3 lbs. 2 oz.
		BALLS: Eclipse (or equivalent).	1 lb.
	Tournament	WICKETS: (Challenge) Winter wrought iron.	2 lbs. each
		1 stake, USCA rules, clips in wooden box.	45–50 lbs. per set
C ($200 to $700)	**Challenge**	MALLETS: Round, Bound or unbound heads, Plain or cord grips.	2–3 lbs.
		BALLS: Composition or boxwood.	12–14 oz.
	Collegiate	WICKETS: (Challenge) Winter wrought iron.	14 oz. to 2 lbs.
		1 stake, USCA rules, clips in box or canvas bag.	30–45 lbs. per set
D ($100 to $300)	**Family**	MALLETS: Round head, Plain wood.	1½–2 lbs.
		BALLS: Composition or Hardwood.	9–14 oz.
	Garden	WICKETS: Light weight Wrought iron or wire.	14 oz.–2 lbs.
		1 stake, USCA rules in box or canvas bag.	20–30 lbs. per set
E ($60 to $150)	**Junior**	MALLETS: Round head, Plain wood.	under 2 lbs.
		BALLS: Composition or Hardwood.	9 oz. (minimum).
		WICKETS: Bent wire.	2 oz. up
		1 stake, boxed.	15–25 lbs. per set

Notes appear on page 68.

Sizes (Dimensions)	Court Sizes and Grass Level	USCA Approved/Recommended and/or Suitable for Use By:
36" shafts 9" × 3" heads 3⅝" diameter ⅝" diameter uprights 3¾"–4 span	105 × 84 feet or scaled down to ½ size Putting green (smooth and level) Flat to ¼" high	Authorized for international championships by Croquet Associations worldwide and all USCA national, regional, sectional tournaments. Interclub, intercollegiate, invitationals, country, golf, tennis clubs, sports clubs and private club play.
33"–36" shafts 3⅝" diameter 7⁄16" diameter uprights 4" span	105 × 84 feet or scaled down to ½ size Fringe (of golf green) ¼"–⅝" high	Country, golf, tennis and sports clubs (Challenge, or winter, wickets are often used on existing putting greens or lawn tennis court surfaces). Collegiate, private club and family play.
33"–36" shafts 3⅝" diameter 5⁄16"–7⁄16" diameter uprights 4" span	105 × 84 feet, or scaled down proportionately to a minimum of 50' × 40' Golf fairway ½" to 1" high	Intracollegiate, interschool (intermediate), informal club and family play.
32"–36" shafts 3¼"–3⅝" diameter up to 5⁄16" diameter uprights 4"–5" span	Scaled down from full size to fit available area Fairway to low rough 1"–1½" high	School, family and beginner play.
28"–33" shafts 3"–3¼" diameter 4"–6" span	50 × 40 feet, or to fit available yard area. Low rough, 1"–2" high	Juniors, children, informal play.

The following accessories are available and, in many instances, are included in the sets:

Clips (blue, red, black and yellow)
Corner flags (same four colors)
Ball markers (same four colors), used to indicate positions on the court when, because of darkness or weather, a game is not completed
Smasher (for driving wickets into the ground)

NOTE: John Jaques & Son, Ltd., manufactures sets in these classes under the following names and USCA classifications:

USCA Class   A—Championship #100 (71000) Association #101 (71010)
USCA Class   B—Club (Roehampton) #102 (71020) Tournament #103 (11030)
USCA Class   C—Challenge #107 (71070) Collegiate #109 (71090), #111 (71110) or #125 (71250)
USCA Class   D—Family #127 (71270) or #120 (71200) Garden #131 (71310)
USCA Class   E—Junior #136 (71360) or #143 (71430)

USCA Class C equipment (Model 3600) is also made by Forster Manufacturing, Wilton, Maine.

Three classes of basic equipment: Proportionate in weight, quality of materials and craftsmanship, components of class "A" "C" and "E" types of sets are, from left to right: (1) "A"-class 3-lb. lignum vitae brass-bound mallet, 6-lb. cast-iron association wicket and 1-lb. composition Eclipse ball; (2) "C"-class 2¼ lb. hardwood mallet, 2-lb. bent steel Challenge wicket and 14-oz. wooden ball; (3) "E"-class 18-oz. rubber-headed mallet, 1½ oz. plastic-coated bent-wire wicket and 9-oz. wooden ball.

6

GRIPS, STANCES AND SWINGS

The Grip

One of the more widely circulated pictures of Diana, Princess of Wales, is a shot of her as a spunky nine-year-old with a croquet mallet in her hand. Judging from the headlines and captions that have accompanied this photograph, the point seems to be that the Princess, in playing at a tender age a game thought to be the exclusive province of titled nobility, was "born to be Queen." As a budding croquet player, however, you will see that the *real* point of the photograph is that Diana is about to use the Solomon grip.

This is a significant piece of information because now that equipment has become more or less standardized, the grip is one of the few parts of the game in which personal preference can be expressed. And while it may seem a cruel irony that, if you are just being introduced to the game, you are confronted with a multitude of ways to hold the mallet, confront them you must. For everything you do later in croquet—from the simplest, 6-inch positioning shot to the most dazzling 80-foot cross-court roquet—flows directly from your ability to swing the mallet naturally and easily.

Every croquet player develops, in time, his favorite grip. That personalized grip is not, then, merely the ratification of an initial choice, but the gradual realization that one grip really produces more successful results than any other. We recommend that you read this chapter with a mallet in hand and, after each description of a grip, hit a few balls using that grip. Later, play a few games with

Princess Diana may eventually enjoy a firm hold on the English throne, but as a child she opted for a left-handed Solomon grip.

the one that feels best. There will probably be some stiffness in your hands at first, but keep at it, periodically reviewing your grip to make sure you haven't, through fatigue or carelessness, let your hands slip into some other position.

How will you know when you've found the grip that's right for you? It's not necessarily when you make a shot that's previously eluded you, or win a game, or elicit questions from even greener players. Rather, it's a process of elimination; one day, having tried Lord knows how many grips, you'll just *know*. There you'll be, standing over a mallet *without* thinking about your grip—and in the perfection of that moment, you'll have found the one that best suits you. In that instant, your mallet will become what you most want it to be: a 3-foot extension of your arms.

Although some of the grips we're about to describe may seem somewhat torturous, these are the grips that have been most widely accepted by players who have been at the game for decades. It may be scant consolation to you as you're twisting your thumbs around a mallet, but these grips are intended to be comfortable. For comfort is the ultimate concept in croquet; if you're standing over your mallet in pain, the studied consciousness that results can only be reflected in your shot.

However personalized the subject of grips may be, there's no reason to go it completely alone. If you're having difficulty and an "A"-level player—or, better yet, one of the game's greats—happens to walk onto your greensward, ask him to watch you hit a few. As in golf, a subtle adjustment in the grip may produce a dramatic improvement in your game.

Finally, whatever grip you choose, there's only one way to hold the mallet—as if it were a soft-boiled egg. Firmness is the key—you don't want to drop your mallet or watch it go sailing out toward the next wicket—but so is a certain tenderness. As Lord Tollemache says, "Remember that you are not holding a sledgehammer, but an instrument of touch." In a game where the best players often look as if they're having trouble staying awake, the hypertense, over-stressed, constricted malleteer doesn't have a chance.

THE STANDARD (AMERICAN) GRIP

Many Americans will find that the most comfortable and effective grip depends on the widest possible separation of the hands. American courts have as much to do with this as anything else. Compared with English greenswards, which are rolled and manicured so frequently that an extraterrestrial, hovering over them, might think he had happened upon a nation of lawn worshippers, our croquet lawns are bumpy and coarse. Consequently, a shot that would, in England, require a mere love tap will, on most American courts, necessitate a stronger stroke.

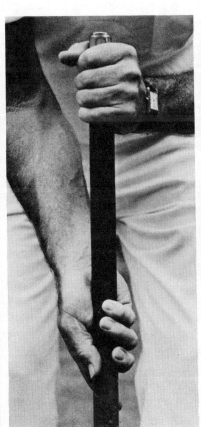

The standard American grip: With this grip, the knuckles of the upper hand face squarely forward. Side view: Notice that the knuckles of the upper hand face forward. Front view: The palm of the lower hand faces forward. Right: The American grip, with "pencil grip" variation.

To try the American grip, the first step is to grip the top of the mallet with your left hand. The easiest way to think of the left hand position is to remember those schoolyard baseball games when the team captains would choose sides. One captain would toss the bat to the other, and, after it was caught, the captains would, by turns, grab the bat, with the winner being the captain who could grip the bat closest to the top of its neck. Skipping the interim steps, that is essentially what you want to do with your left hand: get it comfortably gripped at the top of the mallet without any part of your hand wrapped over the top and with your knuckles facing forward toward your target.

The right hand goes, according to your preference, six to twelve inches below the left. The palm rests against the back side of the octagonal grip, and your index finger should be pointed down along the side or at the back of the mallet. As in other grips, the point is to keep the index finger and the pinky of the right hand from influencing your stroke. The second and third fingers of the right hand are the crucial ones, and if you've correctly positioned your hand, all they do is hold the mallet. If they affect your aim at all, you're doing something wrong.

Another variation of this basic American grip has the lower hand grasping the shaft as if it were a large pencil cupping the handle between the thumb and forefinger with the middle finger down the side and fourth finger against the back. We know of two world-class players who favor this "pencil" grip.

THE STANDARD BRITISH GRIP

This grip is the same as the American grip but with one difference: here the hands touch at the top of the shaft. As your shooting skills improve or as you find better and faster courts to play on, you might consider bringing your hands closer together until you become comfortable with the British style. There is one advantage to this grip, and it is considerable: the closer your hands are to each other, the less either hand can dominate and, in the resulting imbalance, throw off the intended aim or strength of your shot.

Most frequently used with the center stance (for stances see page 80), this grip is often also used in conjunction with the side-style stance with the bottom hand near the upper or slightly below it on the shaft.

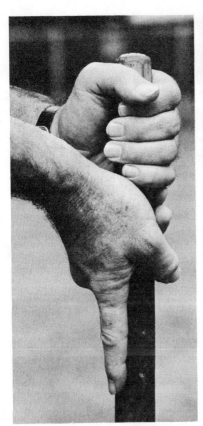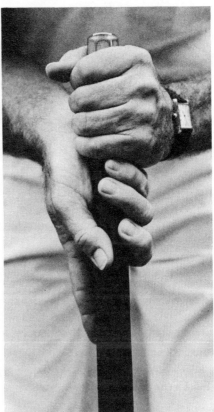

The British standard grip: The hands are held together near the top of the shaft.

THE IRISH GRIP

This grip was introduced by a half-dozen brilliant players from Ireland who dominated the sport in the Edwardian era. It is particularly useful for those players who have trouble with their stroke because one hand exerts more influence than the other and consequently sends every ball off course. With the Irish grip, that error is almost automatically corrected. The hands practically cup the mallet. Both palms face away from the body, and both thumbs rest on the front of the shaft.

When used with a shorter mallet or with the hands set lower on the shaft, the Irish grip seems to increase accuracy—particularly in shots for the wicket at close range. A number of top American players and World Champion Nigel Aspinall favor this grip for that

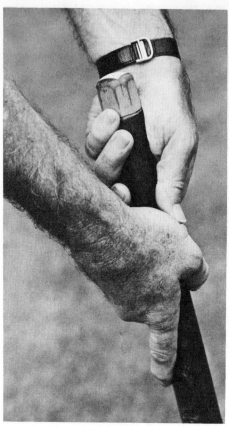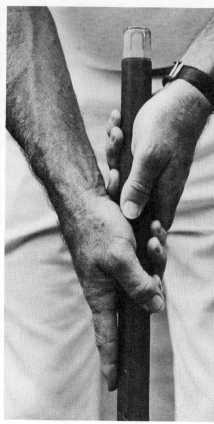

The Irish grip: Here, the hands cup the mallet and are more interlocked than in the other grips.

reason. After a disappointing season a few years ago, however, Aspinall switched to the standard (American) grip for many of his shots and quickly resumed his winning ways. Today he alternates these two grips for various shots, which suggests some latitude is permissible (or desirable) in this area.

THE SOLOMON GRIP

John Solomon recalls that he "invented" this grip as a child because it was simply the only way he could handle a mallet, which was almost as tall as he was. Later, he tried to switch to a more standard grip, but he soon discovered that for roquet shots and shots at the wicket he much preferred his own grip style. With more than fifty English and international titles to his credit, Solomon now includes several top-ranked American players among his devotees. His grip is unusual in that both sets of knuckles face away from the body.

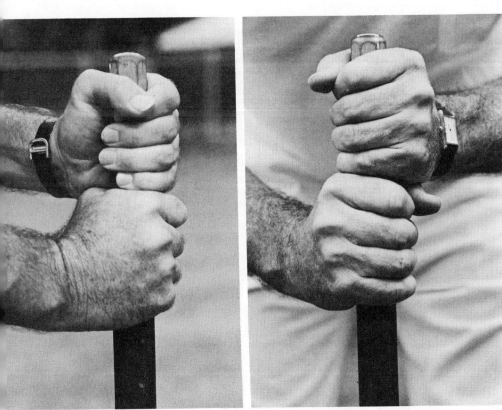

The Solomon grip: In this two-fisted grip, the knuckles of both fists face forward at the top of the handle.

THE SOUTH AFRICAN (OR OSBORN) GRIP

After years of experimentation, Jack Osborn has found a grip that enables him to hold his mallet exactly the same way every time he takes a single-ball stroke and during many of his two-ball strokes. The secret is the upturned thumb: With the pad of the thumb being fixed squarely against the back panel of the octagonal handle, the upper hand can't shift around the shaft. It also guarantees that the left elbow will remain tucked in during the stroke.

The Osborn grip is a modification of the grip used with obvious effectiveness by nine-time South African champion Tom Barlow. Barlow uses a pencil grip with his right hand, which is lower on the

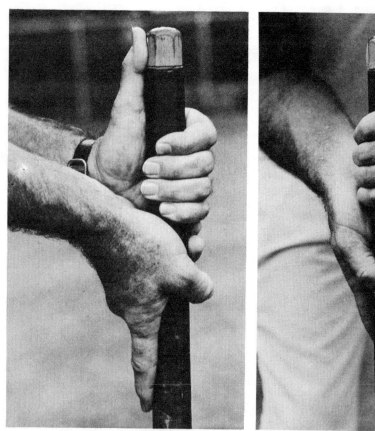
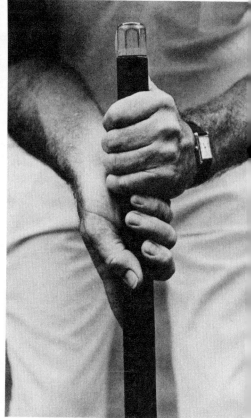

The South African (Osborn) grip: The upturned thumb guarantees consistent upper-hand placement.

shaft. Osborn keeps his right hand next to his left in the standard palm-out grip at the top of the shaft.

He believes that this seemingly minor adjustment from the standard British grip he had settled on in recent years has since his visit to South Africa in 1981 materially sharpened his long roquet and single-ball shots.

THE GOLF GRIP (AND STANCE)

This may be the most natural grip for those who come to croquet from that other lawn sport, but it doesn't work as well on the greensward as it does on the fairway. For croquet is a game that ultimately rests on skills that are demonstrated at relatively short

The golf grip (and stance): As in golf, the palms face each other. The hands may be interlocked.

distances, and the golf grip tends to encourage fantasies of teeing off. Why do we include it at all? Because those whose arms are not strong may want to switch to the golf grip—and the golf stance and swing (see pages 82 and 90)—for long shots. As in the Irish grip, both palms are cupped around the shaft facing each other and both thumbs rest on the top of the shaft. Here, however, the left thumb is almost covered by the right.

In 1872 the cue stroke was outlawed, ending the use of the shot in which the narrow tip of the shaft was held like a billiards cue by a player who was, as often as not, lying on the ground.

In 1899 it was decreed that mallet heads had to be uniform, a crushing blow to those players who carried tiny mallets in their vest pockets for occasions when a regular mallet couldn't advance the fortunes of a hoop-bound ball.

As a result of these two edicts, croquet changed from a game well suited for contortionists to a more civilized and sportsmanlike contest played exclusively by erect bipeds—with the exception of backyard and roque, in which short (10-inch to 18-inch) handles still force the players to assume an inelegant squat or stoop to hit the ball. These edicts are a great boon for the fledgling croquet player, for, in choosing a stance, he must consider basically only three ways to approach a solitary ball that he wishes to hit.

THE CENTER STANCE

For most players, this will be the only stance worth considering. The player stands directly behind the ball. He points in the direction he wishes the ball to go. Neither foot exerts more influence than the other. And in swinging the mallet like a pendulum between his legs, the player has the greatest possibility of sending the ball in the direction he wants it to travel.

The greatest advantage of the center style, however, is that it reduces to a bare minimum the necessity of thinking about your feet and allows you to give more consideration to your arms and grip. Because this relocates all your thought and energy into the wrist, it may cause some soreness in that area the first few times you play, but the advantages of this stance are so great that we urge you not to abandon it for a less-effective though more immediately comfortable style.

If, as you stand behind the ball, you still feel a certain awkwardness, try this stance with one foot slightly ahead of the other and a bit more of your weight on the forward foot.

The center stance: Both Richard Illingworth and his partner, young Kiley Jones, 1981's National Club Team "B" Flight Champions, prefer the center stance.

The center stance (women): As highly ranked Cathy Tankoos demonstrates, women can get additional power and control by standing with one leg back.

Start with your feet shoulder width apart, with your left foot from six inches to eighteen inches in front of your right (if you are right-handed, otherwise the reverse) and aligned with the direction of your target. The weight should be evenly distributed and your knees slightly flexed. Again, comfort is the objective, so you should experiment with the distance your right foot should go back until you feel an even balance. The farther your right foot goes back, the more your weight should shift to the left foot.

Women tend to place their right foot farther back than men, since this stance provides somewhat more leverage during the swing than a more aligned stance. The latter is a variation of the center stance, which, in fact, is favored by many top English male players who keep both feet closer together and at the same level.

THE SIDE STANCE

For those who are taking up croquet after years, or even decades, of physical inactivity, the side stance might prove sensible. Evolving from the era when long dresses prohibited swinging a mallet between the feet by the ladies, the side stance is seldom seen in tournament play today. It offers some of the power of the golf stance and yet delivers most of the control of the center stance. For all that, it is no instant solution to the challenge of standing over the ball without throwing off your aim—in this stance, it's more difficult not to twist the body slightly as you shoot.

To assume the side stance, face the ball and hold the mallet to the side of the foot. Your knees should be slightly bent. If desired, one foot can be moved forward to reduce even further any strain in the back and legs.

THE GOLF STANCE

Those who have graduated to association croquet from backyard competition almost invariably have mastered the golf stance. And with good reason: backyards are often bumpy, and it takes a hefty backswing to advance a ball even a few feet on such a lawn.

On the greensward, however, the golf stance is usually a liability. For one thing, it breaks the flow of the stalk, that apparently seamless series of gestures which enables a player to line up his shot and execute it without breaking stride. For another, it forces you to turn your head to check your aim. In short, it forces you to think at exactly the time when you ought to be finished with thinking.

The side stance: Players with bad backs will find that playing croquet won't aggravate their troubles if they adopt this stance and remember to keep their knees bent.

Despite its drawbacks, the golf stance (see stance in figure on page 91) is well suited for long-distance shots on uneven or heavy lawns. To use it in a single-ball shot, stand at a right angle to the direction you want the ball to travel, taking care that the ball is just inside the left toe. For a long drive or double-ball shot, stand slightly in front of the ball. But no matter what kind of shot, a slow backswing is suggested, and, as you are often told in golf, let the mallet head do the work as you reach the point of impact and on into the follow-through.

Stalking

Jack Nicklaus approaches a golf ball from behind, never from the side. So should you. On the green, Nicklaus looks at the hole, then at the imaginary line from his ball to the hole, and finally at a point on this line about three feet ahead of the ball. You should too. And, like Nicklaus, you should do all this before you are hunched over the ball—during what is known in croquet as "the stalk."

It is difficult to convince neophytes that the most important moment in successful shot-making takes place *before* you swing your mallet and send the ball on its way to its target. And yet that is the absolute truth. As John Solomon points out, you can swing brilliantly, you can hit the ball with the precise degree of force you intend—but if the stance you've taken sends the ball off in the wrong direction, what does all that matter?

That line of aim is decided during those few seconds while you stalk the ball. It is confirmed when you plant your feet and prepare to swing your mallet. Lord Tollemache said he could always tell when a player was going to miss his shot because, instead of shooting at once, he waited two extra heartbeats before taking his swing. In other words, the player was rechecking his angle, readjusting his mallet, looking at the lay of the balls on the court—*thinking*—when nothing should be on his mind but a smooth, slow backswing and an effortless stroke.

The most crucial thing to remember is that you *must* finish your internal strategy session *before* you begin your stalk. Depending on the position of your ball, stand 6 to 12 feet behind your ball, carefully assessing not only where you want the ball to end up, but what your next shot is and, if you happen to miss, what your opponent's probable response will be. Inevitably, if there are two alternatives, there are many more. You cannot, in the interest of completing the game before nightfall, stand there indefinitely as you compute the possibilities; if you're spending more than 30 to 45 seconds considering your options, you're taking too long.

Having decided where you want your ball to end up, consider what kind of shot will produce that result. Draw an imaginary shooting line between your ball and its target point. If you're not standing on that line, move to a place where you are. Then, like Nicklaus, pick a spot a few feet ahead of the ball that's on this shooting line. At this point—and only at this point—should you

The stalk: (1) Stand 6 to 12 feet behind your ball and draw an imaginary line between it and its target. Then (2) walk to your ball, keeping your eye on the shooting line. Finally (3), take a firm but comfortable stance.

stride up to the ball, keeping your eye not on the distant target but on the interim spot on the shooting line.

Theoretically, you're now ready to take your shot. We suggest that you don't. Instead, use your mallet as if it were a gun and the mallet head were a barrel, taking one final practice swing. Let the mallet follow all the way through and then, at the very top of the swing, freeze. Look at the sight line on top of your mallet head. Where it's pointing is where your ball will go.

Now, at last, you're ready to shoot.

The Swing

Students of history with a special fondness for leaders whose lives can be reduced to a single footnote may remember the Duke of Plaza Toro's claim to fame: he led his troops from behind. He never exposed himself to danger, and so it fell to his regiment to make him famous. Which it did by running away at every possible opportunity.

A good croquet player, like a good general, must lead. He must know not only where he wants to send the ball but how to get it there. The crucial issue here is leadership. Translated into croquet terms, this means, simply, that his mallet must do what his arms direct.

If a player swings correctly—with his arms leading and his mallet carrying through—his game may be boring to watch. He will hit the ball, it will go where he wants, and then he will repeat the process, alternating short roquets, short split-shots, and short shots at the wicket. He never takes a dramatic, cross-court, desperation shot that thrills the spectators; he doesn't need to. For he has maintained his dominance—simply by making sure that his arms lead.

"Any analytical approach to the swing will mean that you are not relaxed," Solomon cautions, "and relaxation is the key to being a successful croquet player. It is rather like listening to music—there are two ways of doing it. You can listen to every note and establish its position within the framework of the whole piece, or you can detach yourself from it, letting the music put you in an emotional frame of mind outside yourself. A croquet swing should be like that:

a movement of the arms that is unconsciously performed and results in a perfect swing."

We stand with Solomon here. Croquet is nothing if not an "inner game," and the compartmentalization of any aspect of the enterprise detracts not only from a player's potential pleasure but from his potential success as well. Still, in the interest of helping you avoid some errors as obvious as the Plaza Toro effect, there are a few pointers we can give you in your quest for the perfect—and perfectly natural—swing.

There are basically three ways to swing the mallet in striking a ball, and since we will be referring to these frequently in the following pages, please get them clearly in your mind. They are hitting up, hitting down, and hitting square (or True).

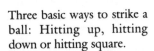

Three basic ways to strike a ball: Hitting up, hitting down or hitting square.

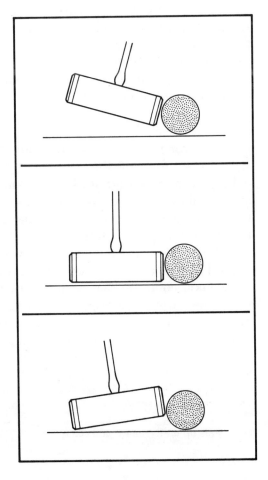

HITTING UP

When striking a single ball, one of the prime concerns is the positioning of your body. If you have taken a stance that leaves you too far from the ball, you will hit the ball as your mallet starts its upswing. The ball, instead of rolling smartly across the lawn, may dribble along the ground like a topped golf shot.

HITTING DOWN

If, on the other hand, you take a stance too close to the ball, you'll be swinging down at the moment of contact. In that case, most of the power of your swing will go into the ground, and the ball may well bounce—or even jump its target.

HITTING SQUARE

When you assume your stance, to hit square, make sure you're situated so the mallet strikes the ball at the bottom of the swing with the mallet head parallel to the ground at impact and with the head carrying ahead smoothly.

There is a fourth way of hitting a ball known in advanced play where one hits with either the left or right side of the mallet head, which is the equivalent of "side" in billiards. The complex aspects of this shot are such that it is rarely used even by experts, and so while the first three swings are *must* techniques for you to learn, we will leave this last for some future treatise.

For the basic square stroke then, another key concern is the movement of your body as you're shooting. Ideally, all movement flows pendulum-like from your shoulders down. Your arms carry the mallet through with little or no wrist action. And that's it. Does your body move? It shouldn't. Does your head snap up to follow the ball as soon as your mallet makes contact? It shouldn't.

Solomon confesses that "it is almost impossible to describe in words how to swing a mallet." We agree. Far better for you to take mallet in hand and work to find your groove, swinging in front of a mirror if you discover you're not getting results. Still, at the risk of

---

The swing: Take a smooth and slow backswing. (1) Swing down from your shoulders (2), not from your wrists. After contact (3), carry the mallet through. Don't look up until contact has been made.

turning you into an analytical player, the following basic precepts can't be repeated often enough:

1) The backswing is slow and smooth, not rapid or jerky.

2) The mallet swings down from the shoulders, not from the wrists.

3) The face of the mallet hits the ball squarely.

4) The mallet does not carry the arms up; the arms carry the mallet through.

5) Look up only after you can see the spot on the grass where the ball lay.

Or, for those who like mnemonics, Solomon offers the following:

*S*talk the ball
*T*ake a comfortable stance
A slow backswing
*N*ever move
*C*arry through
*E*yes down.

Long Shots

There are two ways to get greater distance than is possible from a standard center or side stance. These techniques will be particularly useful for those who have trouble getting power into their shots as well as for those who play on heavy lawns.

THE GOLF SWING

After you assume the golf grip and stance (page 81), the ball should be 12 to 18 inches from your left foot, and, if you are right-handed and swing from left to right, at a point just to the right of your left foot.

THE EXTENDED CENTER STANCE

Here, one leg is set at least one foot behind the other. Like the golf swing, it is not a "perfect" or "natural" technique, but it offers considerably more control than a supercharged swing taken from a classic center stance.

The golf swing: Take a slow backswing (1). Hit just before the end of the downstroke (2). Your body should remain stationary, with your head directly over the ball. Allow your mallet to carry through (3). The mallet should follow the ball's intended path. Look up (4) only when you're well into the carry-through.

7

SHOT-MAKING

Single-Ball Shots

Croquet virtuosity depends on your ability to perform the most basic skill of all—shooting your own ball. Lord Tollemache italicizes this notion: the most difficult thing to do really well, he says, is *to hit your own ball perfectly.* Tollemache's logic is impeccable on this point. The first shot of every turn is, after all, a one-ball shot. With few exceptions, running wickets entails a successful one-ball shot. The final shot of the game—the peg-out—is a single-ball shot.

Obviously, capitalizing on the opportunities presented by successful single-ball shot-making is essential, but you don't get those second shots if you don't take your first shot effectively. And we, like Tollemache, cannot overemphasize this point: *If you could shoot your own ball perfectly every time, you would be virtually unbeatable.*

Not all single-ball shots, however, are made the same way. If you're shooting a wicket, you will take one kind of shot. If you want to hit another ball—to roquet it—you will shoot differently. If you want to roquet that ball to a designated spot, you will vary your shot-making technique yet again. And if, perchance, you are dead on a ball that's in your way, you must attempt one of the more dramatic shots in croquet and loft your ball over your would-be nemesis.

If all this starts to seem intimidatingly complex, it really isn't. What's remarkable about croquet, in fact, is not how many shots you must master to play well but how few. Learn the following single-ball and two-ball shots, use them appropriately, and you'll soon find that you are thinking not about shot-making but about the vastly more rewarding subject of strategy. And then you will learn for yourself what we now propose as gospel: all strategies, from beginner "C" level through expert "A" level, are based as much on your shot-making abilities as they are on your ability to assess your opponent's skill.

The basic single-ball shots are:

> the roquet
> the rush
> the cut rush
> shooting the wicket
> the jump shot

THE ROQUET

The key single-ball shot is the roquet—that is, hitting another ball with your own. The reason it is singularly important is that a successful roquet allows you to earn additional shots, begin a "break" (see page 130) and use other balls as steppingstones as you make your way around the court.

Building on the foundation of the fundamentals of the stalk, stance and swing in the previous chapter, you should now concentrate on the aiming of your ball at a target ball.

At the start of your stalk, draw a mental line straight through the center of both balls and approach your stance directly along the extension of that imaginary line from your ball to you. After reaching your ball, hold your mallet above it for a moment while you recheck the aim by matching the sight line or the top of the mallet with the line running through the balls. Then lower your mallet and your eyes to your ball for the stroke. Take a slow backswing, hit through the ball squarely at the bottom of the swing, looking up only after the ball is well on its way to the target ball. If, after all this, you find yourself missing short roquets, check that you are not looking up too quickly or that your stance is not improperly aligned. These are the most common causes for missing this essential shot.

THE RUSH

Once you have developed some skill in roqueting a ball, you must learn how to rush it—that is, how to roquet your ball into another, sending that ball to a particular spot or in a predetermined direction on the court. At this point, you will quickly understand why some of croquet's better players have been scientists, mathematicians, computer programmers: professional empiricists. For good rushing is nothing but the application of the basics of geometry or physics I—or, for those who turn numb at the mention of science or math, a cheerful willingness to experiment.

As we've explained earlier, good croquet is not a game like golf, where every hole is a fresh confrontation. The player who hangs back, who consolidates his forces and then swoops cunningly through a half-dozen wickets like Sherman closing in on Atlanta, is far more likely to be victorious in croquet than the drudge who concentrates on making each wicket in the fewest number of risky shots. In fact, in the ideal croquet game, a player so arranges the balls on the greensward that he's able to work his way around the court in a single turn. That "all-round break" is the croquet equivalent of a grand-slam home run in baseball.

But imagining yourself accomplishing that rarely seen, beautiful-to-behold feat is folly if you can't send your ball to selected spots, the better to make the next shot, and the next, and the next. You must, therefore, master rushing.

Because he's both dogmatic and poetic, we can't resist quoting Lord Tollemache at length: "The great secret of rushing is to imagine you are actually going to drive the *other* ball with your mallet. There should be an entire absence of any kind of 'jerk' in the stroke. A smooth, sweeping stroke designed to 'brush' the other ball along is the idea to aim at. You should actually regard your own ball as part of the head of the mallet, which is going to brush and sweep the other ball along."

His Lordship is right again, at least on a first-class level lawn. The stroke should be as in the roquet stroke, hit squarely and smoothly with just enough added power to the swing to drive the roqueted ball the distance you want.

If on the other hand the lawn is the least bit rough, you may find it better to hit up in order to avoid jumping over the object ball. Hitting down on any type of lawn is a definite no-no in rushing and is certain to cause your ball to bounce off the top of the object ball, if in fact you don't sail over it completely.

As for the proper aiming line, see diagram opposite.

All too often, newcomers to croquet don't appreciate how exacting a game it is; they don't care where their target ball—their own partner's ball or one of their opponent's balls—stops as long as it's more or less in front of the wicket and not more than 10 feet

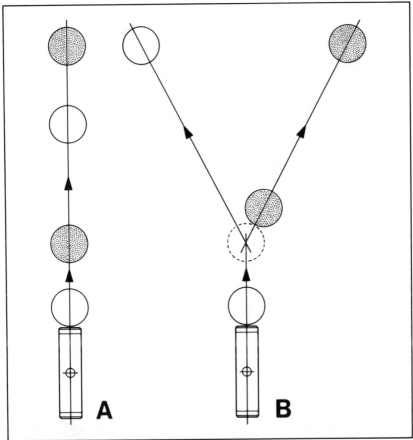

Straight rush and cut rush: Figure *A*: A straight rush sends both balls directly forward. Figure *B*: A cut rush allows the striker to send the roqueted ball at an angle to a pre-determined position.

from it. Experts know better. To the expert, the ideal rush shot puts the target ball 3 feet in front of the wicket and within one foot of its center. Those are, we emphasize, the expert's literal intentions for his shot: to him, 6 feet from the wicket is 3 feet too many.

THE CUT RUSH

Break out your compass. Dust off your protractor. Now it's time to calculate what is known in croquet as the "rush line." That imaginary line between the ball you want to hit and the spot you want to hit it to should suggest the correct shooting angle to you. For pool players and bowlers, this shot is—conceptually, anyway—second nature, and, just looking at a ball that must be sent down-court to the right corner, those players will instinctively know that the roqueted ball must be hit fairly solidly on the left side. See diagram.

When attempting the cut rush, remember that in its fundamentals it's no different from other rush shots. That is, it makes no difference where your ball ends up. Even if it goes off court, you're not penalized. All that matters is getting the roqueted ball to the desired spot and keeping that ball in bounds.

SHOOTING THE WICKET

There you are, directly in front of the wicket with a shot that can't be more than a two-footer. It's a simple, direct shot. You've made more difficult shots a zillion times. You take position. You breathe deeply. You look down at the ball, confirm your aim, keep your eyes down, and finally take what feels like a normal, easy swing. And what happens? The ball *thonks* into an upright and dies there, leaving you not only with the wicket unmade but with an impossible shot on your next turn.

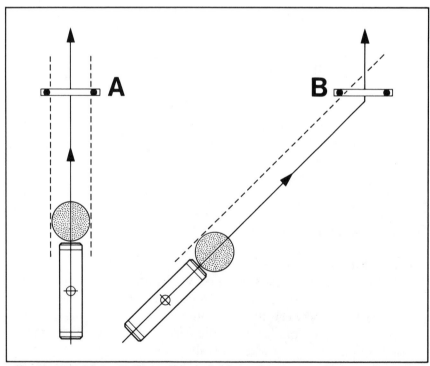

Shooting a wicket: *A:* From directly in front aim at space in center between uprights; *B:* from an angle aim to clear the inside of the nearer upright.

This scenario is every croquet player's nightmare. The ball doesn't always hit an upright; sometimes it hits both and gets hung up in the jaws of the wicket, or, in extreme circumstances, whizzes right by the wicket as if clearing the hoop were the last thing you intended. But whatever the variation, one fundamental truth applies: *When your ball is ready to clear a wicket, you play differently.*

For some players, the reason is an overbearing application of unnecessary strength. They hit without control, substituting power for accuracy. They're looking at the wicket, noticing once again how narrow it seems, and so they say to themselves that if they hit it just a little *harder* than normal, the ball will skid through the wicket before the wicket knows what's happening. But then, to their horror, they learn that in croquet there's no substitute for accuracy.

For other players the problem is a hyperawareness of their tendency to miscalculate their shooting angles. They stalk the ball, take their stance and then, instead of shooting and being done with it, they freeze. Should they leave their stance, stalk the ball again and then take their shot? Or should they put just a bit of topspin on the ball, on the theory that spin will help slide an off-target ball through the uprights? Why anyone who's unsure of his shooting abilities would want to make an uncertain shot even more unlikely is not a question a nervous player asks at that moment. He just shoots and misses.

Or there's the player who comes to croquet from the poolroom, where he's accustomed to rocketing his balls into the pockets— slam, slam, slam. He's not afraid the ball will scour the pocket and jump out, or that his cue ball will break up the pack in a way that works against him. He's fearless, firing hard and true regardless of the risks. In croquet, too, he shoots hard every time, as if his real target is not the wicket but the distant baseline. He may make the wicket, but in the process he loses all control over the final destination of his ball and, more often than not, ends up off the court—or too far away from any other balls to use them to advance or reposition himself.

If even veteran players make these all-too-human mistakes, how can you avoid them? Many observant neophytes avoid them quite well, as it happens—mostly because, in avoiding these mistakes, they make different, and equally dangerous, errors. Most often, when they get near a wicket, they suddenly forget that croquet is a game of controlled aggression. They might have taken a series of fearless shots to get in position, but now they become timid little

Here, in front of the wicket, where players must confront the ...ate test of self-confidence, these players turn into weaklings. ... baby the ball, giving it an unsatisfactory love-tap. On occa-..., they hit the ball so softly they double-tap it, committing an ...gious foul.

The best way to avoid all these errors—plus any others we're all capable of inventing on our own—is to practice shooting wickets at every opportunity until wickets lose their capacity to intimidate you. It's like practicing foul-shooting in basketball or putting in golf: do the right thing often enough in practice conditions and you improve the odds you'll do the right thing in competition.

And don't think just about clearing the wicket; consider where you want your ball to stop on the other side and practice until you can put it within a foot of that spot. To make your practice more realistic, put another ball a few feet beyond the wicket and try to clear the wicket and stop a few inches shy of the other ball.

For straight shots at the wicket, remember the basics of a good stroke.

Concentrate on aiming at the center of the opening.

Take a slow backswing and a smooth stroke.

Let the mallet head carry through; imagine, if you will, that the mallet head will follow the ball through the wicket.

And don't jab or stop the mallet as soon as it makes contact with the ball. An abrupt hit will make the ball skid along the ground for the first 6 to 18 inches before it begins to roll. If that happens, the ball won't have any spin to help pull it through the wicket.

As you become more proficient at shooting wickets straight-on, try skewing the angle to make the shot more difficult. John Solomon has an effective method for clearing wickets from acute angles: he concentrates on just missing the *inside* edge of the *near* upright.

As a general rule, wicket-shooting need not be traumatic if you adopt a custom that some veterans use before *any* shot at the wicket: go around *behind* the wicket and look back through toward the ball. *If you can't see it, you can't shoot it.* In that case, if the game situation permits it, play for position, not for a never-before-seen miracle.

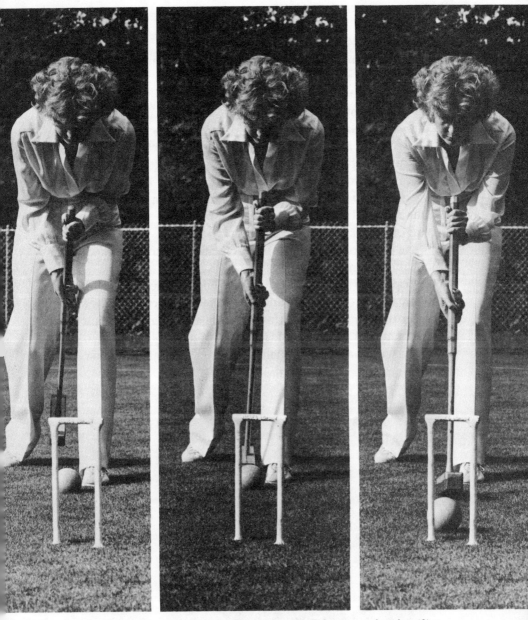

Shooting the wicket: Aim at the center of the wicket (1). Take a smooth swing (2), and, after making contact, carry through (3) as if you're trying to swing your mallet head through the wicket.

THE JUMP SHOT

When you're stymied by another ball or cannot run your wicket because you're obstructed by a ball you are dead on, you may have to attempt what many consider the most dramatic shot in croquet. The jump shot is the favorite of the news paparazzi who can earn combat pay for lying down on the far side of the wicket as your ball soars straight into their Nikon lenses at 60 miles per hour.

It can be achieved with surprisingly little practice by moving your stance forward with the ball parallel to your instep. With hands together, grip low on the handle, carefully aim at the top third of your ball and hit down hard as if to take the top off a soft-boiled egg with one stroke of your mallet.

The ball should literally jump as the force of the mallet squeezes it into the ground on impact.

Properly struck, your mallet should not hit the ground—but since it may while you're mastering it, it is well to practice on the sidelines rather than on the court, thus possibly avoiding unpleasant divots.

Be cautious. It is possible for a ball to jump not only through but over a wicket and occasionally even over the finishing stake.

The jump shot: With the hands held midway down the grip (1), aim for the top third of the ball (2). The mallet makes contact at an angle (3). As the mallet head brushes the lawn (4), the ball jumps over the obstruction.

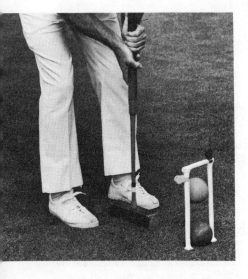

Double-Ball Strokes

THE CROQUET STROKES

One of the best-loved moments in childhood croquet begins when your ball strikes your opponent's with a satisfying *thonk* that elates you and depresses him. Seconds later, he's begging for mercy, but you have none. Taking your ball in hand, you place it directly against his. Then, as if your ball were a bug to be squashed, you plant your foot on it. Having made sure your ball won't budge when you hit it, you smash it so hard that if you miss, your mallet will fracture your foot. But you don't, of course, and your opponent's ball rolls for a hundred feet, ending up perhaps in a rough or on a driveway, from which (because your rules are sadistic) he will

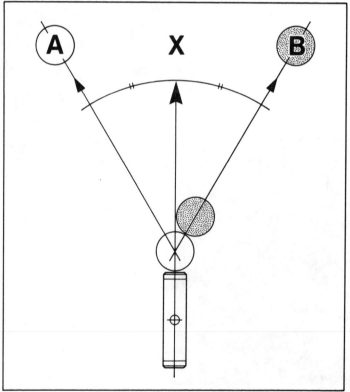

Split-shot: *X* is the aiming point for your mallet when you want your ball to go to *A* and the croqueted ball to go to *B*.

be forced to take his next shot. Not that he gets another turn, for you make an incredible 15-foot shot through the wicket and go on to complete the course before he can even make his way back onto the green.

If that scenario seems too crude and brutish for you, you may remember a different version of croquet's most delicious moment. Disdaining violence after the initial contact, you take your ball in hand and place it a mallet head away from your opponent's ball. You're not going to smash him anywhere; instead, you're going to take *two* strokes, one to position yourself in front of the wicket, the second to clear it as you move relentlessly on toward victory. "Faster, faster!" you cry—as if croquet were a version of Beat the Clock.

In association croquet, we banish all that.

Violence *isn't* sanctioned.

Track spikes *aren't* necessary.

For in association croquet, as in few other sports, strength and speed don't matter. Brains do. So does cunning. An appreciation of mathematics doesn't hurt. And an instinctual understanding of Stoicism is an absolute necessity.

As we keep reminding you, winning croquet rests on your ability to make not single wickets but *breaks*. You hit another ball. You advance it on the croquet stroke to a desired position. You clear the wicket. Then you start the same process again.

In such a game, smashing your opponent's ball into the next county is a useless exercise in machismo. And putting your ball a mallet's head away from your opponent's and leaving that potentially useful ball behind makes just as little sense. Moving your opponent's ball around the greensward with yours, however, is the cornerstone of brilliant croquet. But if you don't master the croquet stroke, you can't make a single break.

The croquet stroke is so easy that it's tempting to describe it in a paragraph and be done with it. After all, what's to say? After you've roqueted the target ball, move your ball in contact with it, setting your ball behind the roqueted ball or at an angle that allows you to hit it to a spot where you can use it again. Make sure the balls are touching and that, when you swing, you don't commit a foul by hitting the roqueted ball. And that's it.

We may sound silly waving our arms and shouting, across this distance, something that should be obvious, but: *You can't control the balls in the croquet stroke unless they're touching*. All too often, a

Preparing to take croquet: Press your thumb under the lip of the roqueted ball (1) and place your ball into the imprint (2).

player makes a successful roquet. He sets his ball next to the target ball. He stalks perfectly. He takes the correct stance. His swing is flawless. And yet the balls don't go where they should. Why? Because although they'd made contact when they were placed together, they didn't stay that way.

If you learn nothing else from this book, learn how to be sure the balls stay together when you're making a double-ball shot: *Before you set your ball next to the roqueted ball, press your thumb under the near lip of the roqueted ball, then lean your ball against it as you put your ball in that imprint.* Your ball will sit in that imprint, and unless gravity reverses itself, the balls will not separate. If you take your stroke correctly, the roqueted ball will move—very little, perhaps, but it will at least shake—and you will have avoided committing a fault.

Still, you're shooting two balls—and that makes you nervous. First, because you might commit a foul by hitting the roqueted ball instead of your own, or by hitting your ball twice, or by pushing your ball instead of hitting it cleanly. Then, too, as with every two-ball shot, you have more than one ball to think about, and that divides your concentration.

As Lord Tollemache points out, if you've lined your balls up correctly, you've already taken half your shot successfully. You've set your ball in proper contact with the roqueted ball, you've stalked the balls to be sure your stance will put you on the desired shooting line—now all you have to do is swing smoothly and hit your ball as described in the following pages. The basic double-ball (croquet) strokes are:

> the drive
> the stop shot
> the rolls (Half, Three-Quarters, Full)
> the take-off
> the split shots (Drive, Stop and Rolls)
> the peel
> the cannon
> the pass roll
> the peg-out

DOUBLE BALL STROKES

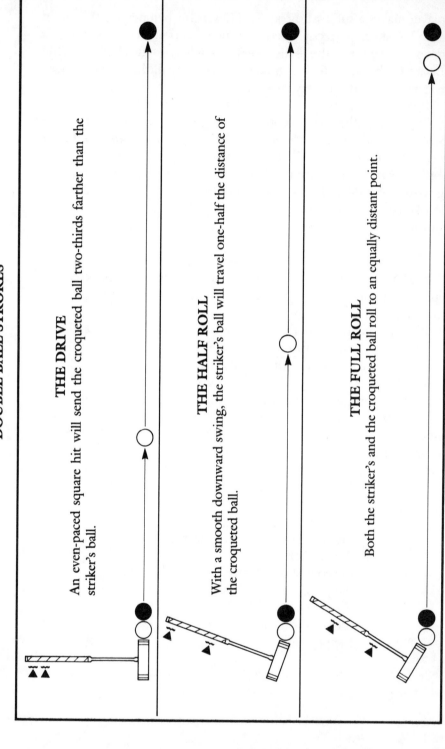

THE DRIVE

An even-paced square hit will send the croqueted ball two-thirds farther than the striker's ball.

THE HALF ROLL

With a smooth downward swing, the striker's ball will travel one-half the distance of the croqueted ball.

THE FULL ROLL

Both the striker's and the croqueted ball roll to an equally distant point.

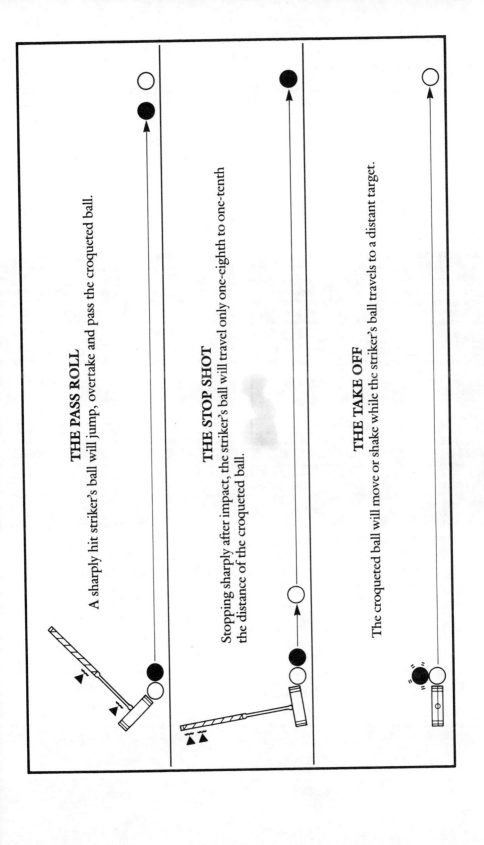

THE PASS ROLL

A sharply hit striker's ball will jump, overtake and pass the croqueted ball.

THE STOP SHOT

Stopping sharply after impact, the striker's ball will travel only one-eighth to one-tenth the distance of the croqueted ball.

THE TAKE OFF

The croqueted ball will move or shake while the striker's ball travels to a distant target.

THE DRIVE SHOT

The drive is the keystone of the croquet strokes. It is the only double-ball shot in which you assume a normal upright stance, swing true, hit your ball squarely at the bottom of the pendulum and carry through as you would on a single-ball stroke. Aim along the imaginary line drawn through both balls to the target spot for the forward ball, put sufficient power into your natural swing to move that ball to that spot, avoid hitting either up or down at contact and that's it. Because, in the drive shot, you hit squarely

The drive shot: Assume an upright position for your mallet (1) and take a slow backswing (2). The longer the drive, the higher you should bring your mallet in its backswing (3). Take a clean swing (4) along the line of aim, hitting squarely at the bottom of the swing (5) and carry through.

with an ordinary swing, it is an excellent stroke for testing what your mallet will do for you on a given lawn.

Whether you are attempting a short or long drive, the forward or croqueted ball should travel two-thirds farther than your own ball. With that as your basic yardstick, all other croquet strokes will produce either more or less distance between your ball and the croqueted ball, as we shall see in the rolls and stop shots.

THE STOP SHOT

If you're playing well, you'll have organized the court so that the balls are all ahead of the one you're shooting. In this constellation, you should be able to keep them in front of you—and to keep them together as you move them around the greensward, clearing wicket after wicket with your ball in the process. The shot most better players find crucial to this feat is the stop shot.

The point of the stop shot is to move your ball as little as possible while sending your target ball far downfield. Experts can make the target ball travel 8 to 10 times farther than theirs. You can, too.

The first step to success with the stop shot is just that—a step. Backward, in this case, so you're about 3 inches behind the spot you'd be in had you assumed a normal stance. Why are these few inches crucial? Because, in order to hit the ball, you will now be forced to bring up the toe of the mallet. You will, additionally, find yourself pressing the heel of the mallet against the ground as you shoot.

The stop shot: Having taken a step back from your usual stance, take a short backswing (1). As you swing, loosen your grip slightly (2), making sure that you jam the heel of your mallet into the ground as it makes contact with the ball (3). There is no follow-through (4) in this shot, so all the force of your swing will go into the forward ball.

The effect of this simple change in your stance is that you won't so much stroke the ball as jab it. Loosen the grip you take on the handle and immediately after impact with the ball drive the heel of the mallet into the ground. Because of this and your altered stance, you'll have virtually no follow-through. That's fine. If you've done this shot correctly, a graceful follow-through is all but impossible.

When the stop shot is made correctly, your ball will do what your mallet does—stop short—and all the force of your stroke will be transferred to the croqueted ball. If your ball rolls more than a few feet, however, something's wrong. Check your grip. It's probable that you're tightening your hands just as you shoot, and that the energy you're putting into the mallet shaft has negated the effects of your altered stance and shortened stroke. If your hands are not the problem, check your stance to be sure you're sufficiently far from the ball. A stroke that doesn't hit up on the ball won't give you the crisp shot you need.

THE ROLL SHOTS

The drive shot, taken from a normal stance, will carry your ball one-third the distance of the croqueted ball. The stop shot will send your ball only one-eighth to one-tenth the distance the croqueted ball travels. Obviously, then, any of an infinite number of distances can be achieved by changing one's stance, grip, angle of mallet and downward stroke during the swing. In the diagrams and photos you will see how these shots can produce rolls that will move your ball from one-half to three-quarters to the full distance of the croqueted ball.

For each roll from the half-roll to pass roll you will note that the

The half-roll: Shift your weight and the angle of your mallet shaft forward (1) and, with your weight still forward, take a slow, smooth backswing (2). Hit down, striking the top third of the ball (3) with a smooth forward stroke and carry the mallet through (4).

feet, weight and top of the mallet shift forward and the hands are placed lower on the mallet shaft and the knees flex more and more as the distance the balls are to travel increases.

For the dramatic pass roll you can see that the lower hand is almost to the mallet head, while the upper is at midshaft. The stroke is down on the top of the ball with a sharp but smooth follow-through.

One caution you should observe, however, is a tendency to over-roll an approach to a wicket, leaving your ball no chance at running the wicket on your continuation stroke.

The full-roll: With the hands lower on the shaft (1), the angle of the mallet is increasingly forward and the right leg is extended (2), with the weight on the forward foot. Take a relatively short backswing and hit down (3) with a sharp but smooth stroke.

The pass-roll: With his right hand almost on the bottom of the shaft (1), Ted Prentis stands with his weight and mallet directly over the ball. He takes a short backswing (2), keeping his weight forward. He strokes down (3), hitting the top third of the ball, making sure to carry his mallet through (4).

THE TAKE-OFF SHOT

There is an exception to the rule that when you are shooting you should never look at any other ball but your own. It is called the "take-off shot," and it is very difficult. It is also necessary, and, although we do not always do it correctly ourselves, we will tell you how to do it.

The take-off shot is actually less difficult to make than it is to see. Your intention is to move the ball you are about to take croquet on hardly at all—and yet to move your ball as much as 100 feet. The thinnest of split shots, it carries with it a certain danger—namely, that you'll make it too thin, and instead of just rattling or shaking the croqueted ball, you won't move it at all.

In croquet the striker is also the referee. It is up to you to notice if you've made the croqueted ball move. You must, therefore, watch it in addition to watching your own ball. The croqueted ball doesn't have to move its position—as long as it shakes, you've proved that the balls were in contact.

On backyard courses, where it's often difficult to keep the balls together in the best of circumstances, it may seem self-defeating to try a shot that requires this much finesse. Still, we urge you to attempt it. You may not always play in bumpy backyards; when you do get the opportunity to play on a tournament-quality lawn and

The take-off: Make sure the balls are touching (1).

Then check to be sure that the "V" created by the tangent of the two balls points in the direction you want your ball to travel by laying your mallet flush against both balls (2) so that the shaft points to your target. To be certain the roqueted ball will move or shake, aim your mallet head (3) on a line pointing slightly toward the roqueted ball.

Swing directly along that line (4) as if the roqueted ball didn't exist (5), with enough force to reach your target.

the occasion calls for a take-off shot, you will unsettle—even, unhinge—an opponent if you confidently step forward and execute a take-off.

SPLIT SHOTS

Not every croquet stroke requires a straight-ahead shot. If you have roqueted the target ball to a point about three feet in front of the wicket and a few feet to one side, in fact, you will want to take croquet with an angled or split shot. For the intention of your next three shots is obvious. First, you will want your ball to have a clear shot at the wicket. You will then want to run the wicket. Finally, you'll want to roquet the other ball you've split to the far side and move on.

The means of accomplishing this are right at hand, in the form of the ball you've just expertly roqueted. All you have to do is place your ball against that ball and take croquet, sending the croqueted

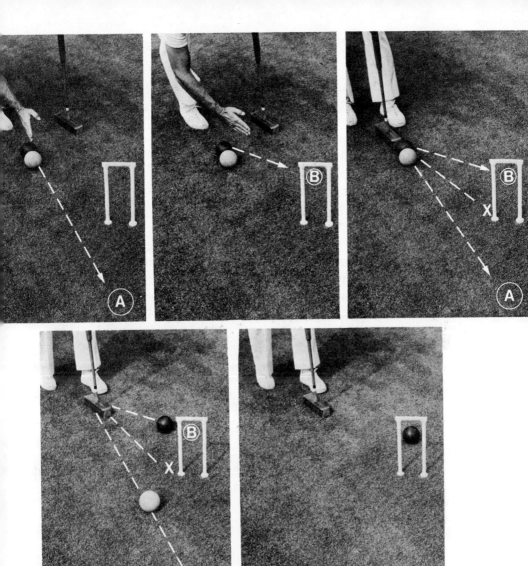

The split shot: Place your ball behind the roqueted ball (1) is such a way that a line drawn through both balls would extend to the spot where you want the roqueted ball to end up (point A). In this case, point A is on the far side of the wicket and slightly to one side. Then envision the direction of a line to the spot (2) where you want your ball to end up (point B). These two imaginary lines create a "V." Aim your mallet (3) at the midpoint of that V (point X). In this case Point X is just to the right of the nearest upright of the wicket. Consciously avoid "steering" the stroke as you swing smoothly along the imaginary line to Point X. In this case, the forward ball is to travel three times farther than the shooter's ball, and a drive shot was used. But no matter the desired distance, each ball should travel (4) along its respective imaginary line. Your ball ends up at point B—in this case, right in front of the wicket (5), which makes it a simple matter to clear the wicket on the continuation stroke.

ball to the far side of the wicket, while leaving yourself a short straight shot at the wicket. The method of achieving this and all other split strokes is to aim your mallet at a point midway between where you wish the two balls to go and stroke along that line of aim. See diagram, page 102. If your shot is properly calibrated and executed, you'll be well positioned to clear the wicket on the next shot. Having cleared the wicket, you will be in a position to make the next roquet. Continuing your turn with another split-shot, you may continue to advance your ball around the course—wicket after wicket after wicket.

There are two factors to consider in making the split-shot: the angle of the shot and the force of the mallet. You can take out your protractor and pocket calculator at this point, or you can go outside, set up a wicket and practice the split shot until you instinctively know the correct angle/strength relationship. We recommend the latter approach.

A book can be of some help, though. As billiards players know, *when two balls are touching and an angled shot is indicated, the balls will split at twice the calibrated angle.* A shot taken beyond a 45-degree angle doesn't, however, increase the angle of divergence beyond 90 degrees. What happens, instead, is that less force passes into the forward ball and it doesn't travel as far. At these angles, we're not talking about split shots any more, but about the takeoff.

These shots are essential to a game built around setting up and maintaining breaks. With this in mind, the names of the following strokes are self-descriptive:

The Split Drive

Normal stance and hit the ball squarely at the bottom of the swing, but aim as in a split shot.

The Sharp or Stop Split

Stand back 3 inches and hit up as in a stop shot, but again aim at the point midway between the target points where you wish both balls to go.

The Split Roll

Your weight and the top of the mallet should be forward and you should hit down on the ball aiming as in the split stroke.

The Split Pass Roll

The downward angle of the stroke is increased and the wider the split, the easier the stroke need be since there is less weight resistance in the forward ball.

THE PEEL

Named after Walter Peel, the object of this stroke is to drive the croqueted ball, and occasionally both balls, through a wicket.

This is particularly helpful when the ball being peeled is your partner's ball, which has accumulated some deadness.

If by luck or skill you manage to roquet the object ball into position in front of the wicket, take your ball and carefully place it so that you can visualize parallel lines running along each side of both balls' pass between the uprights of the wicket. You'll do well to look at this alignment from both sides of the wicket before shooting.

Then, assuming you are not closer than a few inches from the mouth, stop-shot the forward ball through the wicket and then run the wicket with your own ball on your second or continuation stroke. If both balls are within a few inches of the wicket, you may prefer to roll-shot both through on your croquet stroke.

There are occasions when your next wicket is not the same wicket as that of the ball you are peeling. In these instances, you will find it useful to attempt a split or roll stroke as you peel the forward ball while sending your ball to another spot on the court before taking your continuation stroke.

The peel: Make sure the balls are touching (1) . . .

. . . and then imagine parallel lines on both sides of the balls (2) which lead directly through the wicket. Stop-shot your ball (3) so that the roqueted ball clears the wicket. Your ball should end up (4) in position so you can send it through the wicket on the continuation stroke.

In this event, care must be taken to account for an inward pull exerted when splitting two balls. Align the balls with a slightly wider angle to compensate for this pull for a split shot or attempt more of a roll stroke, which provides somewhat more follow for the croqueted ball. Here again, practice makes perfect.

THE CANNON SHOT

There are basically two kinds of cannon shots. One involves making a roquet in the same stroke as a croquet stroke and is more frequently used in the British than in the American game. British laws allow two or more balls to be placed in contact along the boundary line or in the corners. The object is to send the ball you are about to take croquet on and the ball your ball is about to roquet to different spots on the lawn in one stroke. In the USCA game this situation rarely occurs on or near the boundary lines because rules call for a separation between balls. It does occur occasionally out on the court.

The other type of cannon is useful when you wish to move a ball upon which your ball is dead (and thus cannot hit it directly with yours) by hitting (cannoning) another ball into it. Here, the object is to move the ball in the jaws of the wicket by cannoning it with the ball the striker has just roqueted or rushed to a spot nearby. If the two balls are carefully lined up so as to have the forward ball glance off the blocking ball in the croquet stroke, the striker's ball can be left in a position to clear that wicket on his second or continuation stroke. It is permissible that the ball being used to cannon away the target ball may itself be dead on that ball.

This form of cannon, which is often overlooked by even class "A" players, can be effectively used in a variety of other situations on the court, not just with a blocked wicket.

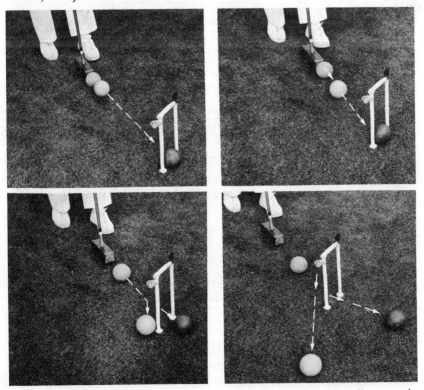

The cannon: After carefully positioning the balls (1) so an imaginary line extends through them to the targeted ball (the ball in the jaws of the hoop), take a stop shot. The roqueted ball rolls smartly (2) toward its target, hits the target ball (3) and knocks it through the wicket, enabling you to clear the wicket (4) on your continuation stroke.

8

STRATEGY

We have said that the key to successful strategic planning rests in your ability to assess accurately the level of your own shot-making and tactical skills as well as those of your opponents.

With this in mind, each shot you take should be weighed in terms of how much you will gain if the shot succeeds against how much you will be giving away if it fails.

If all this sounds like the description of a course in tactical warfare at West Point, you're on the right track . . . for croquet is, in fact, a warlike game.

Along with the basic objective of scoring the 26 points first, each team or player (in singles) should employ those offensive or defensive moves that will restrict the progress of the opponents.

The primary offensive tactic is to utilize as many balls (both partner's and opponent's) as can be brought into setting up what is called a "break" in order to score as many wicket points in one turn as possible. By skillful use and placement of two or three other balls at wickets ahead of the striker's next wicket in proper sequence, the striker can make up to eleven wickets in one "all around break" during one turn. The ability to pick up and maintain a break is, as we shall learn in the following pages, the very heart of offensive strategy.

A key defensive tactic is separating the balls your opponent is playing. Another is taking your opponent out of position to make his next wicket, particularly when his ball is dead on his partner's ball. An opponent who is dead on two or three balls and can be kept that way has lost considerable offensive capabilities. Defensive strategy frequently aims toward placing your and your partner's balls on the boundary line far from the opponents to avoid providing them an opportunity to pick up a break for their side. This move often baffles spectators since it appears that no one is attempting to go for wicket points.

The more experienced player may choose more aggressive tactics, including enticing the less experienced opponent into taking shots that leave him on the field and vulnerable to being used to the advantage of the cagier player.

Remember, however, that it would be futile to master advanced strategy without the ability and confidence to make advanced shots. The challenge of croquet is in mastering and balancing mental and physical skills.

Openings

In American croquet all balls are dead on all other balls until that first wicket is cleared. As a result, there are two basic opening patterns to consider at this point. Assuming that all balls are being played by equally talented players (either singles or doubles), we'll start with the blue ball from one yard in front of the #1 wicket.

In diagram 1, blue clears the first wicket, then goes to the corner behind the #2 wicket.

Red clears the first wicket, in diagram 2, then goes parallel to or slightly behind the #1 wicket, but off the court on the West boundary.

OPENINGS

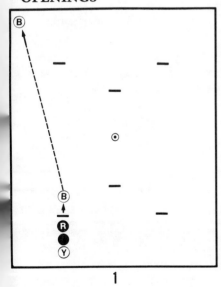

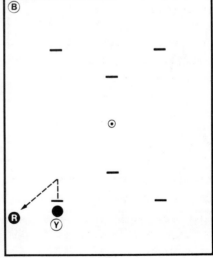

1   2

In diagram 3, black clears the first wicket, then gives blue a rush by shooting to a point between blue's corner position and the #2 wicket.

Yellow clears the first wicket (diagram 4). Now yellow has two choices, the most ambitious of which occurs if black has left himself more than a few feet out on the court. Yellow might do well to shoot at red. In this case, after yellow safely roquets red, it would then take off to black in the second corner in order to send it back to red and then stymie itself from being hit by the blue ball by going behind the #2 wicket (not shown). More commonly, however, and as we have illustrated here, yellow will go out of bounds a foot North of red, so that red will have a good rush upcourt on its next turn.

At the end of their first turn, it's fairly common for the balls to be in the positions shown in diagram 4. It's then usual for the following tactics to be used on the second turn:

Blue roquets (rushes) black to the front of wicket #2 (diagram 5). Then, with a split-shot, blue sends black to the right of the wicket (diagram 6), blue clears the wicket (diagram 7), then rushes black to behind the #3 wicket (diagram 8).

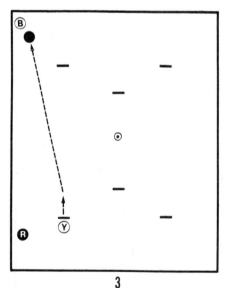

3

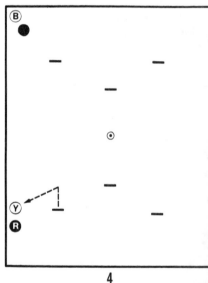

4

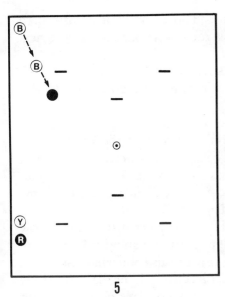

5

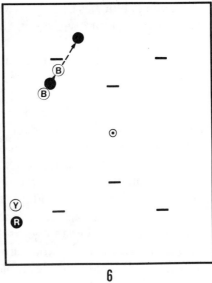

6

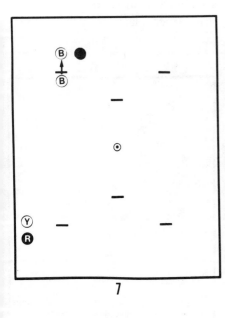

7

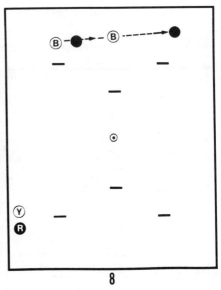

8

In effect, blue has begun a "two-ball break" and is in a position to make two or more wickets in this turn as we shall see in the next section on Breaks.

But let's assume, as sometimes happens, that blue fails to split black far enough behind the #2 wicket to get a good rush to #3. What then?

As common sense demands, blue clears the wicket, but instead of shooting at black, it could go off the court in the third corner (diagram 9) to avoid leaving two balls on the court for the red ball, which plays next, to shoot at. Or, as we illustrate here (diagram 10), blue can tap black, leaving it at the #2 wicket, and take off to yellow and red on the West boundary (diagram 11).

Blue could then tap yellow and on its croquet stroke send yellow to black at #2 wicket and go itself to position behind #3 wicket on its continuation stroke (diagram 12). In this somewhat risky play, blue has achieved two desirable objectives: 1) he has effectively separated the opponents, leaving red, who plays next, a difficult long shot upfield at black and yellow (with luck, blue would have not left them too close together, giving red a double target); and 2) by going to #3 wicket, he sets up an opportunity for black to begin a "three ball" break after making its #2 wicket off yellow. The risk, of course, is that if red hits in on either black or yellow the

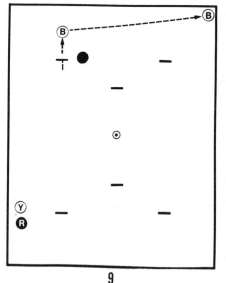

9

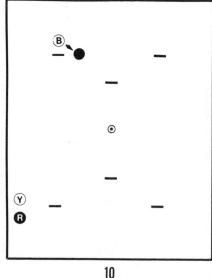

10

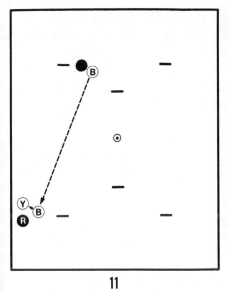
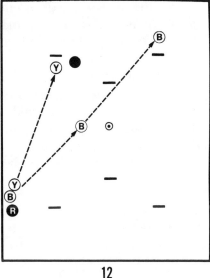

11   12

advantage and opportunity for a "break" shifts dramatically to the red/yellow side, since the hit will have been made at red's next wicket and blue is two-ball dead at #3.

There are other alternatives open to blue in this opening including attempting to get a rush on yellow to #3 wicket instead of sending it to black, but that requires yet another higher level of risk and shot-making skill than the last example.

From here, it's too difficult to imagine, much less describe, the opening alternatives available to each player. The strategic permutations are one factor. But beyond that intellectual challenge is the other, more crucial determinant. That is, as we've said before, the shot-making ability of each player. Clearly, you would be more cautious against a good shooting opponent and not leave him many long, let alone short, shots.

From the spectator's point of view, the way to determine how much respect the players have for one another is to watch where they leave their balls at the end of their turn. When a player brings his balls together at a distant baseline time after time, you know he fears his opponent. On the other hand, when a strong shooter is doing battle with a less-than-stellar opponent, he may well decide to end his turn by leaving his ball at enticingly close range, or even at his wicket, the better to lure his opponent onto center court.

That moment—the equivalent of the moment when a matador bends to one knee before a snorting bull—is often the decisive one in a croquet game. For, if the weaker player misses, leaving his ball exposed, the stronger player can convert that steppingstone into making four or five wickets on his next turn. When that occurs, the virtual equality of field position created by these traditional American openings disappears and—just minutes after the opening shots—it would appear that our matador is certain to be awarded the tail and ears of the loser . . . but as we will see, that is never a certainty until the last ball of the winning side is against the peg.

Breaks

There is a breed of croquet player whose strategy is simplicity itself. Which is to say, a nonstrategy: the aim of this player is to clear the next wicket, and, having achieved that, to race to the baseline and hide. With apologies to feminists, this player, in croquet slang, is derisively known as "Aunt Emma."

It is certain that an Aunt Emma has, at some point in the history of croquet, won a game, but the annals do not record this victory. Nor should they. For Aunt Emma is exactly the kind of player the game doesn't need. Aunt Emma doesn't really want to win—*HE* wants the other player to lose.

Playing against an Aunt Emma can be tedium itself, for he lowers the game to a search-and-destroy exercise. But nothing is worse than two Aunt Emmas on a single court. Croquet is a game of confrontation, rewarding courage and faith. Two cowards attempting to have sport with one another is not croquet. And yet, unless your teachers and opponents force you to develop aggressive shot-making strategies, you will, for a time, become an Aunt Emma.

What fearful beginners and permanent Aunt Emmas don't want to confront is nothing more terrifying than the idea of making two, three or four wickets in a single turn with the help of the three other balls—in other words, making a break. This resistance to breaks is silly, for the seemingly effortless flow from wicket to wicket that a successful break makes possible is the very essence of winning croquet. Like the passing shot in tennis or the tee shot to the green in golf, a good break is a thing of beauty. Better yet, it is within your grasp.

One reason players shy away from attempting breaks is that the break which is easiest to describe and visualize—the two-ball break—happens to be the most difficult to execute.

Still, let's start with the two-ball break, with the understanding that precision placement is crucial. Here, as in the two-ball, three-ball and four-ball break, it's essential that you keep the target ball ahead of you. Your ball should function as a kind of broom, sweeping the target ball ahead of you so you can use it to your advantage on subsequent shots. Picking up where we left blue and black at the #3 wicket (diagram 8 on page 127), black has been successfully rushed to a spot 3 feet in front of the wicket on the approach side and 1 foot off to the side from its center (diagram 1).

Having diligently practiced rushing, however, you won't find it an insurmountable challenge to advance the target ball to the designated spot near the wicket. On your next shot—the croquet stroke (diagram 2)—you are thus able to plan two shots ahead. First, you want your ball to end up in front of the wicket, giving you a clear shot through the uprights. Second, you want to move the croqueted ball to a point about 6 feet beyond #3 between it and #4

The Two-Ball Break

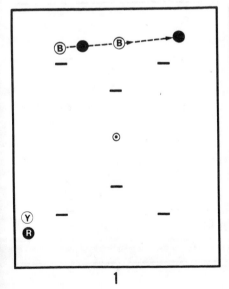
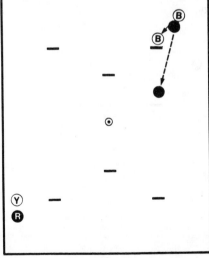

1   2

(diagram 3). This position is important, for after you've cleared #3, you'll want to have a clear rush shot to advance the target ball to #4 wicket (diagram 4).

How do you accomplish all this with a single shot? Very easily, as it happens. You simply make the shot which is the basic building block of successful break-making—the split shot.

Blue now splits black 2 feet past and 1 foot to the right of #4 (diagram 5), runs the wicket with control so that blue has a rush on black to #5 wicket (diagram 6) and on its croquet stroke splits black 6 feet beyond the #5 and itself to position on the approach side of the wicket (diagram 7). Then after running the #5 wicket, blue again rushes black up to the #6 wicket (diagram 8), splits black past and to the left of #6 (diagram 9), and after running #6 is in position to rush black to the 1-back wicket (diagram 10).

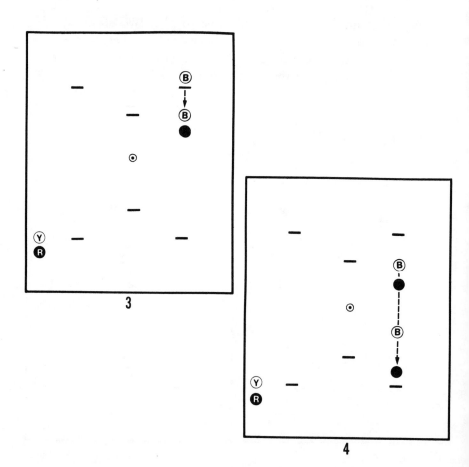

3

4

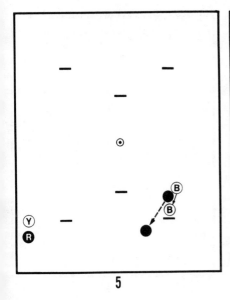

5

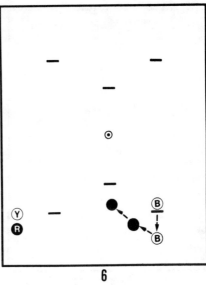

6

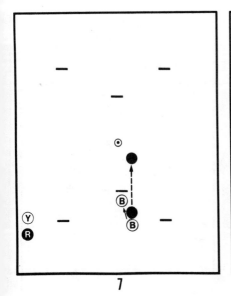

7

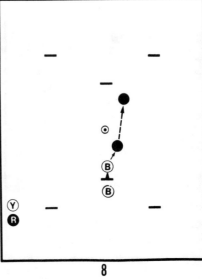

8

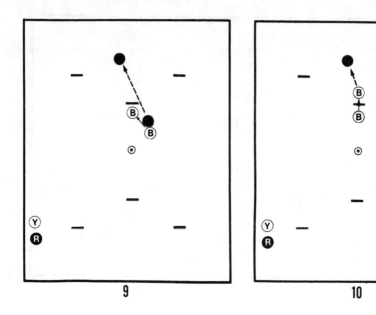

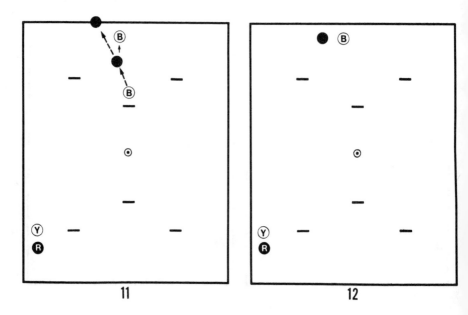

Blue has now successfully scored four wickets in this two-ball break (not counting the #2 wicket in the Openings section) and conceivably could continue all the way around the course of wickets. But as luck (and an errant shot) would have it, blue rushes black off the court, thus ending his turn (diagram 11).

At this point, however, we want to address the question of strategic range. Assuming that you learn to make perfect split shots, should you split the balls, clear the wicket, rush the target ball to the next wicket, split the balls again, clear the next wicket, and so on, all the way around the court? Should you, in other words, perfect the two-ball break to the exclusion of all others?

No. You may take a two-ball break around the court. That would be an impressive achievement, a testimony to your inspired shooting and cool nerves. But for all its brilliance, the sustained two-ball break doesn't represent brilliant strategic thinking. The reason is simple: to sustain a two-ball break, you must ignore every other ball on the court. If you were playing solitary croquet that would be no problem, but unfortunately for the player addicted to the two-ball break, there is always an opponent waiting for his turn, knowing that the two-ball break can end with the slightest miscue. As we have just seen, such a situation occurred when blue accidentally rushed black off the court and thus ended its turn.

Wittgenstein said, "The limits of language are the limits of life." Ditto in croquet. If your strategic vocabulary is limited, you can't expect to see as much—or shoot as well—as better-endowed players. You must, therefore, be constantly vigilant to detect any weaknesses in your own game as well as to learn from other players.

If you are a true croquet player, this vigilance will be one of the attractions of the game. Croquet is, after all, not a terrifically physical sport. Strength scarcely matters. As long as you can stand, you have enough endurance. But a propensity for Machiavellian scheming, a willingness to prey on your opponent's weaknesses, and the fortitude to hang tough in a difficult situation and force it, by will and intellect, to bend your way—these are the hallmarks of every great croquet player's approach to the game.

Such a player understands very well that association croquet is not just backyard croquet with different equipment. Croquet is not a version of miniature golf. And it is not, courtesy of the two-ball break, a form of leapfrog. For the skillful player, the entire court is his to dominate. For him, the idea of the game seems to be to shoot at everything *except* the next wicket. And yet, at endgame, it is, more often than not, this player who gobbles up a half-dozen wickets to take the victory.

By what method does such a player achieve all this?

By mastering the three-ball break.

For what this player has come to understand is something you too will quickly discover: Making a two-ball break all the way around the court is a very dicey proposition. At some point, you *must* pick up more balls. Only by using every ball on the greensward do you have any hope of fending off your opponent and—almost as an afterthought—achieving victory.

The Three-Ball Break

With blue and black on the North boundary as the result of blue's breakdown during his two-ball break, we begin the red/yellow side's turn with the balls in diagram 12. For his patience red is now in a position to pick up a three-ball break with a bit of courageous shooting starting with the rushing of yellow up the lawn toward #2 wicket (diagram 13).

Instead of splitting yellow to the right of the #2 wicket (as blue had done earlier with black in starting his two-ball break), he splits it to the left (diagram 14), runs the wicket and then rushes yellow toward the second corner (diagram 15). At first glance, it appears he

THE THREE-BALL BREAK

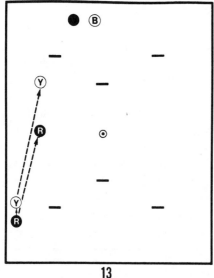

13

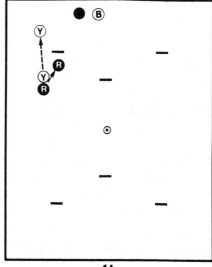

14

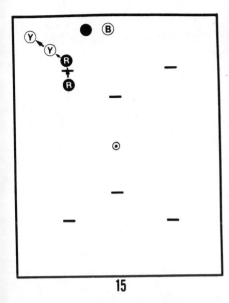

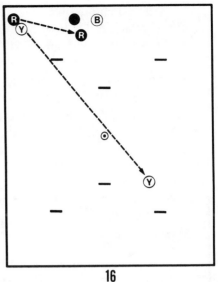

15   16

has forgotten that he is for #3 wicket across the court. Not so—for in order to establish the three-ball break he must get a ball across and down the court *near* #4, while at the same time picking up the black or blue ball on the North boundary. This risky maneuver requires a split shot with a stop-shot stroke that stops his ball near black and blue, while yellow is sent almost to #4 (diagram 16).

Red then softly roquets black (diagram 17), and on his croquet

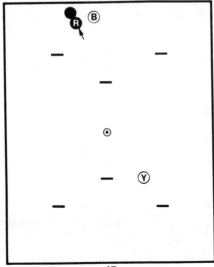

17

stroke gets behind blue (diagram 18) in order to rush it to #3 wicket, which red is now for (diagram 19). After splitting blue to the far side of #3 (diagram 20) and running the wicket, he softly roquets blue a few feet (diagram 21) and takes croquet with blue aimed to go to the approach side of #5 wicket (diagram 22) and in the stroke stops his ball with a rush on yellow to #4 wicket (diagram 23). After hitting and then splitting yellow to the far side of #4, red runs the wicket so that he can roquet yellow again softly (diagram 24).

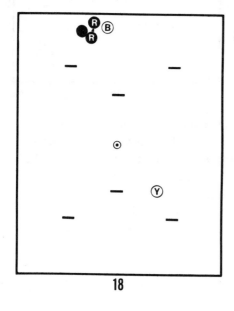

18

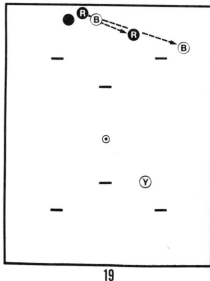

19

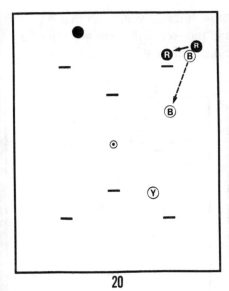

20

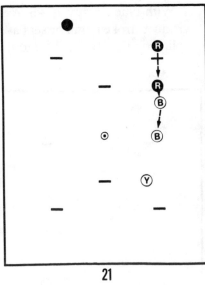

21

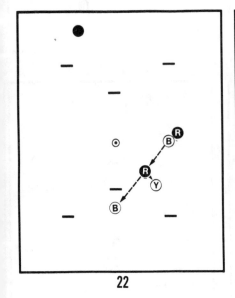

22

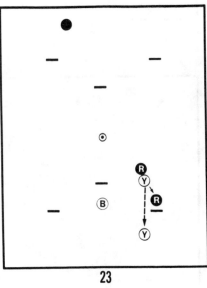

23

With blue already at #5, red now lines up yellow so that on his croquet stroke it will be sent as the "pioneer" ball up to #6 while his split stop shot brings him to the blue ball at #5 (diagram 25).

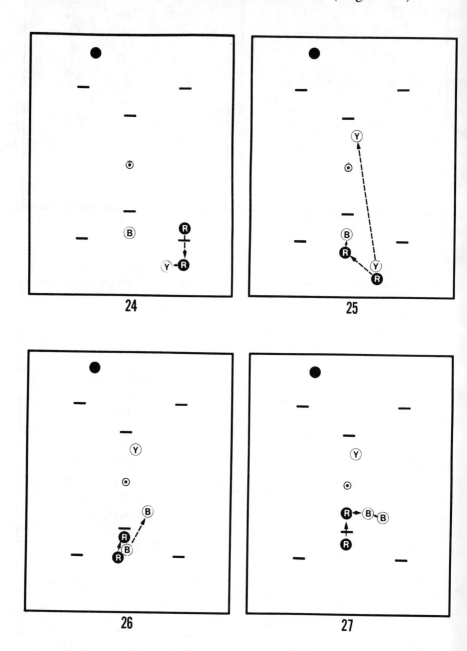

24

25

26

27

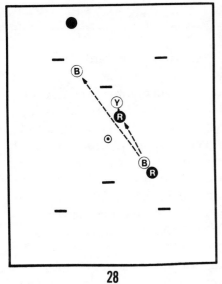

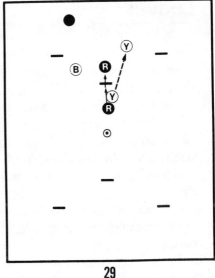

28   29

After roqueting blue, red splits it to the right of #5 wicket (diagram 26) and runs the wicket with control in order to roquet blue again (diagram 27). He then aims the blue to a point between the #6 and 1-back wickets and plays a half-roll shot, stopping his ball close enough to roquet yellow, which is waiting at #6 (diagram 28).

At this point, you can see that after using the three balls in making four wickets so far in this turn, red is now in a position to pick up the fourth ball (black) after running the sixth wicket (diagram 29).

The success of the three-ball break rests in keeping the "pioneer" ball ahead and in front of the next wicket your ball will be for after it makes the one you are now for (or as the English say, the next wicket but one).

By adding the fourth ball to the task of making multiple hoops in one turn, break-making is made much easier. We will examine how this can be accomplished in chapter 9, Exercises and Drills.

Leaves

Unlikely as it may seem as you're clearing your third wicket and bearing down on the fourth like Bruce Sutter throwing fastballs with two out in a late inning, your turn will eventually end. At that point your opponent will step onto the greensward and attempt to rout you as you are, even now, trying to rout him. This is invariably an unhappy moment. It can, however, be made less unhappy if you've given him nothing much to shoot at.

Knowing when your turn is going to end is a little like knowing the hour of your death; you're sure to miscalculate. Where you end your turn is, in reality, the byproduct of more variables than anybody can generalize about, but one broad truth must be remembered.

Do not be tempted to leave either of your balls out on the court or at a wicket unless both balls of your opponent are dead on them or they are dead on each other. To do so will surely invite him to attack and remove that ball or send it back to his partner ball to set up a break for his side.

If you have managed to keep control of your break, you should plan to separate your opponent's balls, preferably by leaving or sending the one that shoots after your partner ball to that spot near your partner's next wicket. You then join up with your partner at some safe distance from the next opponent ball to shoot. This "divide and conquer" tactic combines the best of both defensive and offensive strategies in one play and can be employed frequently throughout a match.

One other sensible way to end your turn, paradoxically, is to do just as Aunt Emma would—shoot for the boundary. Better yet, shoot for a point on that baseline a few feet from your partner ball.

The argument for what may seem to a novice to be a cowardly and boring shot is simply that you don't want to become a steppingstone for your opponent. If you go to the boundary and your opponent comes after you, the odds are good that he'll be attempting an approach shot of considerable distance. He may well miss. If he does, and you're not dead on his ball or your partner ball, you'll have a splendid opportunity to pick up a two-ball or three-ball break.

But even if your opponent does manage to make contact with your ball, he'll be taking croquet from the boundary. Unless you've left your balls too close together or one a few feet out on the court, he will not be able to get in to get a rush for his next wicket or another ball. Still, he may be foolish enough to try for a long boundary shot. And, because the odds are against him, he may end up with a bad leave for his pains.

If he's any kind of strategist, however, your opponent won't attempt any of the above. Instead, he'll do exactly as you've done; respecting your shot-making ability, he'll keep his distance and shoot for a distant boundary line. What may then ensue is not the kind of thing that dazzles spectators—you hit your next ball a few inches down the baseline, he taps his ball a few inches along his baselines in an effort to set up a good rush or tempt you to attack, until finally someone makes the mistake of giving the other player an opportunity by leaving a ball on the court.

If you find yourself resisting this style of play, you will probably benefit from a few games in which you don't shoot for the boundary. They will probably be very short. You will probably lose. And then perhaps you will understand why veterans try to keep their opponent's balls as widely separated as possible; try to keep their opponent's balls wired or stymied from all but a distant ball; and try to end their turns with their own balls together at a distant baseline in preparation for the break they intend to start on their next turn.

End of Game and Pegging Out

The sweetest sound a croquet player can hear comes at the end of a hard-fought game. Having cleared the rover wicket with both balls and having shot one of them against the peg, the soon-to-be-victorious player sends the last ball against the peg with a resounding thud. It all seems so inevitable: it's late afternoon, the shadows are deepening, there's no breeze. This is a moment out of Fitzgerald, out of Waugh, and somehow you know that it will be followed by icy drinks, much laughter, a shockingly expensive dinner, perhaps even a spot of late-night wickedness.

Yes, it is a beautiful moment. There is, however, one small problem—it's not inevitable. All too often, a player on the verge of victory hears that final thud of his opponent's ball against the stake *before* he takes his final shot.

As we've pointed out, one of the greatest similarities between croquet and life is that it's possible to lose at any moment. In other sports, such constant vigilance isn't required. In basketball or football, for example, a team that's leading by 40 points in the last quarter is virtually guaranteed the victory. Even if its opponent hears the voice of God and becomes divinely inspired, the clock militates against a comeback.

But in croquet, a player can be seemingly out of the match when one careless shot by the opponent, usually the result of mounting nervous tension, can completely turn the tide as the opponent "snatches defeat from the jaws of victory."

The most common way for your side to finish after the second ball clears the rover wicket is by rushing the partner rover ball to the stake and on the croquet stroke knocking that ball against the peg, and then your own.

Preferably this will be done just after your second ball has run the rover hoop, but if you're widely separated from the partner ball you must join up with it on some boundary line to set up a rush for one or the other of your balls (depending on their respective deadness) back to the finishing peg on a subsequent turn.

Should you fail to get a good rush on your partner to the peg, another tactic would be to roquet your partner and take off to the opponent ball that follows your partner's ball in sequence. After roqueting the opponent's ball, you send it back to your partner ball on the croquet stroke, and, on your continuation stroke, go to the peg.

All of this assumes your partner's ball is alive both on the ball you have just sent him and on yours. If you have been careful not to give the opponent's ball that now follows you too good a shot, and he misses, your partner then roquets the other opponent ball you've kindly delivered him, takes off to get a good rush on your ball near the peg, and after roqueting you closer, pegs out first your ball then his own ball for the win. If, however, your balls are dead on one another, you have fewer choices. You can shoot at a ball on which you are alive and use your croquet and continuation strokes to get to the peg, or you can shoot directly at the peg.

9

EXERCISES AND DRILLS

Over the years, the USCA has conducted a number of croquet clinics to help beginners develop their playing skills. Recently three of the top teachers of the game in America and England—Professor Xandra (Sandy) Kayden of Cambridge, Massachusetts, who is Vice-President and Director of the USCA Collegiate Division; Teddy Prentis, USCA Tournament Director, multiple title holder and first professional croquet instructor at the Palm Beach Polo and Country Club; and England's G. Nigel Aspinall—collaborated in putting together a set of exercises and drills. Their students responded enthusiastically, and, with thanks to Professor Kayden for turning them into crisp prose, we commend them to you.

The object of the following set of drills is to enable you to reach the point where you can make most of the shots used in croquet with comfort. There is no shortcut to achieving that end except practice, but if you think of each exercise as a game and compete against yourself or another player, you may find these drills surprisingly pleasant.

Single-Ball Drills

TOUCH SHOTS—PLAYING TO A SPECIFIC SPOT

One of the most difficult things to judge in croquet is just how hard to hit the ball to get it into position to make a wicket or to the other side of the court. This exercise is designed to improve your sense of touch in distance shooting.

Begin with four balls lined up next to each other on the north or south boundaries. Hit the first one a few inches in, the second a little further, and so on until all four balls have been struck to form a diagonal line into the court with the fourth ball at the end of the line farthest in toward the opposite boundary. Pick up the first three balls, and using the remaining fourth ball as your starting point, continue hitting the balls from the boundary further down the court. Each ball should stop just beyond the one before it. If you undershoot, retrieve that ball and shoot over until it lands in the proper place. The premium in this exercise is in the greater number of strokes it takes to cross the court. You should be able to do it in forty or fifty strokes. Fewer strokes would mean you are less accurate in your placements.

RUSH SHOTS

The object of the exercise is to develop control in rushing. Using two balls, place one a foot in front of the other on the north or south boundary. Softly rush the forward ball a few feet so that the ball you are hitting remains behind it in position to rush it again. The goal of the exercise is to rush the forward ball down the court without picking up your ball or moving the ball in front other than by the rush. In order to maintain control of where the balls land, you should not try to cover too much ground at one time. If you "cut" the rush (i.e., hit the forward ball on either the left or right side instead of squarely in the middle), you will find the forward ball moving to the right or left of your ball. You can regain control of the forward thrust by cutting your rush back the other way. It should take forty to fifty strokes to cover the length of a full-sized court.

Double-Ball Drills

SPLIT SHOTS AROUND THE WICKET

The goal of this exercise is to improve your sense of how much split and how much stop, drive or roll you need in order to control both balls in a croquet stroke at the wicket. Using eight balls, place them (two each) in a 180-degree arc 3 feet from the wicket. Aim them in such a way as to place your ball in position 18 inches in front of the wicket and located by a marker (you may use a coin for this) and the forward ball to a marker you have placed 5 feet on the far side of the wicket. Repeat the exercise on the other side of the wicket, still aiming for the same positions.

STOP AND ROLL SHOTS

These shots from stop to full rolls—and the infinite variations in between—are the most common croquet shots in the game. The *stop shot* is frequently used to place the striker's ball in position in front of a wicket and the forward ball on the other side of the wicket in position to continue play once the striker clears the wicket. A stronger hit—often called a "beefy" stop shot—is the mainstay of three or four ball breaks as the forward ball is sent to pioneer position at the next hoop but one, and the striker's ball is sent either to a pivot ball in the center of the court or a ball at the next wicket.

The exercise should train the shooter in the differences between the stop and roll shots. Beginning at the boundary line behind one of the corner wickets, stop-shot a ball so that the forward ball lands near the wicket and your ball stays as close as possible to the boundary. Repeat the play with a drive shot, with the forward ball to the wicket and your ball one-third the distance. Repeat it again with a half roll, then a three-quarter and finally a full roll, bringing both balls to the wicket.

Practice making long shots by repeating the exercise from the north or south boundary, sending the forward ball to the nearest center wicket, and then the farthest center wicket. Repeat the shot two more times, and by increasing the roll each time, bring your back ball closer to the wicket without letting the forward ball move much beyond it.

For long half-roll shot practice, begin at the center on the boundary line, aiming the forward ball to the nearest center wicket and the striker's ball to end level with the corner wicket. Next shoot the forward ball to the stake and the striker's ball level with the nearest center wicket. The third exercise should send the forward ball to the corner wicket diagonally across the court and the striker's ball level with the peg.

The Split-Roll Shots

As with other split shots, the roll is used both for delicate wicket shots and long shots to set up or maintain a break. At the wicket, it is frequently used to place both the striker's and his partner's balls in position.

Beginning at the boundary line in a corner, roll both balls to position at the wicket as in the earlier split drill. Repeat the exercise from side boundary. Be careful in each of these shots to split the roll to assure a clear shot with the striker's ball through the wicket on the continuation.

For long split rolls, begin again in the corner and roll your ball to position at the center wicket and the forward ball to the peg. From here, pick your own targets and increase the width of the splits and the distances to be covered.

WICKETS AND BOUNDARY SHOTS

There are numerous other exercises, such as shooting a wicket from different distances and angles. One can never overpractice wicket-running. We suggest that you start from relatively close in, and, as you develop an ability to make the wicket consistently from that distance, gradually increase the length of your attempts.

Another good exercise is to place your ball at various distances from a boundary and shoot at balls a mallet head in from that boundary. The trick is to make sure that neither ball goes out of bounds. This "touch shot" can only be mastered by repeated practice.

Perhaps the most productive exercise we know of is the four-ball break. As described below, this is the one execise that brings all of the shots previously described into play in a drill you can truly enjoy as you learn—and which will improve your game with each attempt.

The Four-Ball Break

If you have attempted to master the two- and three-ball breaks and have had some difficulty, breathe easier, for we have saved the best for last.

With the four-ball break we introduce an exercise that is not only instructive but also great fun.

THE FOUR-BALL BREAK

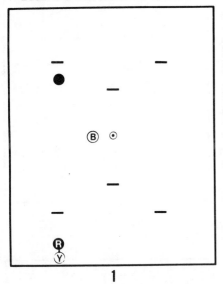

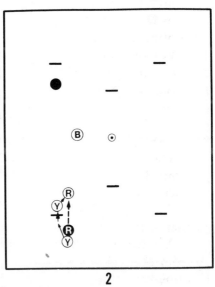

1   2

To begin, place the black ball 3 feet in front of #2 wicket and the blue ball 6 feet to the left of the center stake.

Now place the red ball a foot in front of yellow, which is one mallet head in from the boundary behind wicket #1 (diagram 1).

You are playing yellow. Start the break by rushing red to about 3 feet on the approach side of the first wicket, then split red to the right and about 5 feet in front of the wicket. Run the wicket on your continuation shot (diagram 2).

Now looking up the court we see the black "pioneer" ball waiting at #2 wicket and the blue at the pivotal spot by the peg—but no ball at #3, which will be needed after making #2. After softly roqueting red, you line up the croquet shot so that it will go to #3. Instead of a long split shot to get yellow up to #2, you have the relatively easier option of making a straight-ahead half-roll shot, stopping your ball near blue at the peg while red goes to the third wicket (diagram 3).

You now softly roquet blue and in the croquet stroke take off to black at the second. In the process you will split blue somewhere between the peg and the sixth wicket (diagram 4).

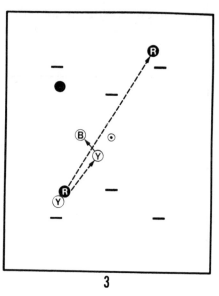

3

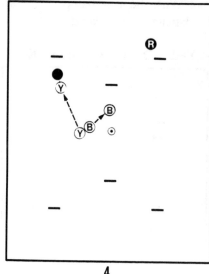

4

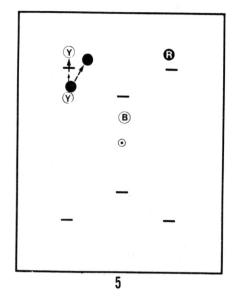

5

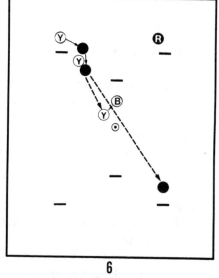

6

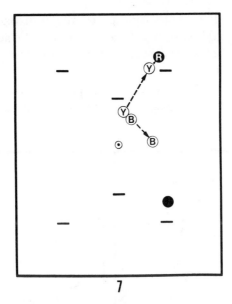

7

After roqueting and splitting black to the far right side of #2, you run the wicket (diagram 5) and gently roquet black again. With another hefty half-roll, send black to #4 and you (yellow) to blue at the pivot in mid court (diagram 6).

By now you will realize that using the pivot ball in these straight-on half-roll shots is *far* easier than the pinpoint rushing required in the two-ball break or the wide split shots needed in the three-ball break.

So again you softly roquet the blue ball and take off to red at the third, splitting the blue ball slightly to the east of the peg this time (diagram 7). By moving the blue pivot ball around the peg to the side of the court where your next wicket is your next roll shot will find it in more or less a straight line with where you will be sending the next "pioneer" ball.

In this case after making the third wicket off red (diagram 8), then roqueting it, you will be sending it to the far side of #5 wicket with your half roll bringing you once again back to blue (diagram 9).

From here the whole concept of the four-ball break should become clear and you should be able to repeat the action of sending the "pioneer" ball to the next wicket but the one you are for and using the "pivot" ball to ease the way.

This of course looks easier on paper than on the lawn so in practice sessions take a bisque each time a shot fails. By counting the

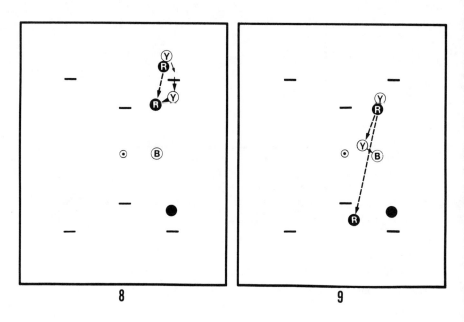

8   9

number of these bisques needed to make all twelve wickets, you can measure your improvement after each exercise.

Once you've mastered the four-ball break, why not practice a three-ball version by simply setting up the start the same way but eliminating the pivot ball at the peg. You'll soon appreciate the value of learning and practicing how to pick up and maneuver *all* the balls into your breaks.

The Croquetathlon

The British Association and the USCA have devised several croquet exercises that we have found to be extremely helpful to both beginning and veteran players alike and particularly useful to those clubs that wish to inspire more active and rewarding play for their members. One such exercise that adds in the interest-retaining element of competition is the croquetathlon.

The croquetathlon allows a large number of players to participate on limited court space and attempt shots which are essential to the game. The events are designed to offer a basic understanding of the various shots required in playing a real game while offering a fun, competitive exercise to novice and champion alike.

A player may compete in a croquetathlon individually, as a member of a team, or both. Teams should consist of two or three players (four players per team tends to slow the pace). Each team should have a balance of a more experienced player with a less experienced player or players. Two teams should be paired with each other to compete in the same events at the same time in order to keep each other's scores. Each team has a captain to keep the other team's score, and players of each team take alternate turns rather than each player taking three or five attempts at one event in a row. It's particularly important in the last event that a member of the opposing team keeps the stroke count of a competing player. To facilitate posting of scores, a tournament director should have a list of all players grouped by teams and a space to mark the individual event scores for each player.

The longer version of the croquetathlon takes about 3 hours for eight three-man teams per court, with several events taking place on one court at a time. The shorter version takes about two hours. While court positions for events 1 through 4 can vary, the last event requires all of the court and must be played last.

USCA members clubs use it both for introducing new members to the various shots of the game and for allowing its membership to compete on a large scale in one four-hour-long event.

RULES OF THE CROQUETATHLON
LONG VERSION

Event 1

Five attempts at shooting a hoop from a distance of fifteen feet directly in line with the hoop.

Points Awarded for:

Hanging ball in jaws of hoop (touchable by straight edge down nonplaying side of hoop—use edge of mallet's head)	1 point
Clearly running hoop (not touchable from playing side of hoop)	2 points
Total possible event points	10 points

Event 2

Set one ball a mallet head's distance from a corner wicket on the peg side. Set another ball directly in line with the wicket one mallet head in from the boundary line. Take five attempts at shooting the wicket, ending as near to the ball on the boundary line as possible without going out of bounds. Roquet that ball without knocking it out-of-bounds. Then take two shots from the roqueted ball and attempt to make the middle wicket closest to the hoop just made.

Points Awarded for:

Making hoop and no roquet	0 points
Making hoop and roqueting out of bounds	1 point
Making hoop, roquet and not making the next hoop	2 points
Making hoop, roquet and next hoop	3 points
Total possible event points	15 points

Event 3

Five attempts at shooting at a ball placed one mallet's length in front of a corner hoop from a mallet's head in from the nearest side line. After hitting it, you are to split the roqueted ball, and after making the corner hoop, roquet the other ball again. Then take your two earned shots and make the closest middle hoop.

Points Awarded for:

Making roquet and not hoop	1 point
Making roquet, split shot and corner hoop	2 points
Making roquet, split and both hoops	3 points
Total possible event points	15 points

Event 4
Five attempts shooting at the center stake from side boundary.

Points Awarded for:

Within one mallet's length from stake	1 point
Within one mallet's grip length of stake	2 points
Hitting stake	3 points
Total possible event points	15 points

Event 5
In as few strokes as possible, each player plays one ball through the 12-wicket, one-stake course from start to finish counting strokes. Par is 35; in the event that the player's score is over 35 the net result will be a minus number to be subtracted from the player's total score of the preceding events. In the case of a player scoring lower than 35 the net result will be added to the player's total score.

CROQUETATHLON
SHORT VERSION

Event 1
Same as long version only three attempts are made. Possible 6 points total.

Event 2
Same as long version except only three attempts are made. Possible 9 points total.

Event 3
Same as Event 4 of longer version except player makes only three attempts. Total possible event points, 9.

Event 4
Same as Event 5 except only 6-wickets and stake are scored. Par is 17.

Total all the scores to determine the winner. The individual or team with the most points wins the competition.

10
VARIATIONS

Over the past eighty years countless variations of the game of croquet have evolved in America. The predominant spinoff is roque (pronounced as in "broke"). Roque was first played in 1899, when the British croquet association outlawed mallets with rubber tips on one end of the head and metal or an equally hard substance on the other end. Angered by this ruling, the Americans who headed the National Croquet Association dropped the *c* at the beginning and the *t* at the end, and "croquet" became "roque." It was this transformation of the game that, more than any other factor, guaranteed America's descent to the cellar in the world of international croquet.

Roque was introduced as an Olympic sport at the 1904 St. Louis Olympiad, where the gold medal was, inevitably, won by an American. But roque's first appearance as an international sport was also its last. It continued to prosper in America, particularly during the Depression, when the WPA installed hundreds of clay-and-sand courts bordered by concrete in the Midwest and South. Roque is still played today under the auspices of the American Roque League, last known to be headquartered in Dallas, Texas.

Unfortunately for the cause of association croquet, many Americans still confuse roque with croquet. In parts of Kentucky, for example, roque is played on clay courts with short (10- to 18-inch) rubber-and-metal-headed mallets under the auspices and rules of the Kentucky Croquet Association.

Roque and the countless other variations of croquet—"Robber" and "Polo Croquet" being the most widely known—succeeded in muddying the American croquet scene and encouraged manufacturers and players alike to create their own interpretations of the game. While all this was going on, however, the rest of the English-speaking world was, under English Croquet Association laws, refining and consolidating its game and the quality of its equipment.

It is instructive to consider the roque-and-croquet career of Archie Burchfield of Stamping Ground, Kentucky. Frequent winners of the Kentucky championships, Archie and his son Mark modified their roque mallets to conform to international standards, learned the 6-wicket USCA rules, and, in their first attempt at a national title, won the 1982 USCA Doubles Championship in New York. Clearly, succeeding at association croquet is possible for those who have started their croquet careers playing what the USCA considers a "variation" of the game.

Those who have learned their 6-wicket lessons well, however, are sometimes not immune to the charms of variety. Of the many variations, the USCA endorses only two: British 6-wicket croquet, as set forth in the rules of the Croquet Association, Hurlingham Club, London, and a traditional favorite played in both countries, golf croquet.

Golf Croquet

The one variation of the game that seems to have successfully crossed international boundaries and with only minor differences in starting position or court layout can in fact be played competitively by one and all throughout the world. This is golf croquet.

Until recently it was played in America primarily on 9-wicket, 2-stake court settings on lawns measuring 200 by 70 feet. And mostly it was played in two places: in Old Black Point in Connecticut and on 6-wicket, 1-peg courts in Hobe Sound and Johns Island, both in Florida. Pronounced crow-key by its practitioners, its popularity undoubtedly rests on the fact that it is relatively easy to learn and thus provides beginners with a game they can enjoy almost immediately.

The USCA has found golf croquet an effective introductory exercise for large groups of beginners; it encourages its clubs to teach and play this variation competitively in "C"-level tournaments until those new players move up to the association game.

Many Americans and British top players enjoy playing this variation when time precludes a full association match.

In England the winners of their annual Golf Croquet Championships are most frequently those you will also find in the British Open and Presidents Cup finals.

So what is golf croquet?

First of all, golf croquet is *not* real croquet; it is a steppingstone towards croquet. It's about as different from association croquet as checkers is from chess. Though many of the movements are similar and similar equipment is used, the tactics of the two games are far removed in both interest and complexity. Why then do we bother to explain it?

First, because it is a good introduction to a croquet court and it teaches the sequence of wickets, which is the same as in association croquet.

Second, it gives excellent practice in some of the basic strokes of croquet, such as running the wicket and rushing. It also teaches the neophyte how to play with control—that is, to play a ball to a chosen spot.

Here the similarity between croquet and golf croquet ends. For the croquet shot itself, which is the characteristic shot of association croquet, is not used in golf croquet at all.

Golf croquet is a game in which the winner of a wicket is the side that makes that wicket in the fewest number of strokes. The similarity with golf is that everyone is going for the same wicket at any one time. The important difference is that the balls are allowed to interfere with each other.

The balls are paired as in croquet—red with yellow and blue with black—and doubles or singles may be played. A point is scored when one side manages to run a wicket in order with either of its balls; the winning side in a timed game is that which has scored the more points at the end of a game. If a short game is being played, the number of points is 7 and these consist of six wickets as in croquet, followed by wicket number 3 if a decider is needed. For a middle-length game, 13 points are played; in this case the six wickets are played twice and wicket 3 is the decider should there be a tie after 12.

The balls are played strictly in sequence—blue, red, black, and yellow. Unlike croquet, there are no extra shots and turns. For example, if red makes a wicket all players then turn their attention to the next wicket and black has the first shot in approaching that wicket.

There are several rules that differ from those of croquet. First, it often happens that in trying to run a wicket the ball gets stuck in the "jaws"—that is, it starts to run the wicket but does not get completely through. In this case, it must be hit back to the playing side of the wicket on its next turn before that wicket is again attempted. If, however, it was placed in that position by an opponent's stroke, the ball may then on its turn continue straight through to score the point. A ball may also score the point by being rushed through the wicket by either side.

Secondly, a player may not anticipate the running of a wicket by deliberately going on to the next hoop.

Thirdly, jump shots, where the ball leaves the ground, are not allowed. This rule is intended to protect the lawn from possible damage and also to make the stymie a useful tactic. The rules for golf croquet may be found on page 203.

11

TOURNAMENTS

USCA tournaments range in scope from small one-day "at home" events to what has become the biggest annual croquet event, the USCA National Club Team Championship. This event is held in conjunction with the U.S. International Challenge Cup, which pits the top USCA players against an International Team each spring in Palm Beach.

In 1982 these combined tournaments drew almost 120 competitors from thirty clubs for a week-long event that included a Black Tie Croquet Ball (white sneakers optional).

What makes the National Club Team Championships attractive is the fact that each member club (depending on size) may enter from one to six teams to compete at any level from beginner/novice (C), intermediate (B) or expert (A) for a national title.

Many newer clubs enter "C" teams for the opportunity it provides them for learning more about the game in general, while competing at a peer-group level.

The second-largest tournament is the USCA National Singles and Doubles Championships, held each September in New York City. The 1982 event was the Sixth Nationals and was limited to the 64 top players from five regions who were determined by regional rankings (and play-offs, where required).

USCA regional tournaments such as the Southern Divisional at Pinehurst, North Carolina, Central at Bourbonnais, Illinois, New England at the Newport Casino in Rhode Island, and Pacific in San Francisco were launched in 1982. These regional tournaments provide clubs in those geographic areas access to top-flight competition, which can lead to the National Championship level. In the 1982 Nationals, thirty-two entries in each of the singles and doubles events were allowed to play in the five-day-long tournament on four courts in New York's Central Park.

Far and away, however, the heaviest tournament action takes place within member clubs' internal competitions—some clubs have as many as five tournaments a year—and the popular Invitationals, where host clubs invite members of other clubs to compete with and/or against their members.

While the USCA recognizes several tournament formats—single elimination, round robins, etc.—we strongly recommend the standard double elimination format.

The double elimination tournament allows each player or team to play at least two matches. Thus, should a player lose one match, he or she is still capable of winning the tournament. The USCA Nationals and regional championship tournaments employ the double elimination format.

As in the case of a straight single elimination, the top four players or teams are seeded. Note that losers of upper-bracket matches play other losers until a final winner of the lower bracket then plays the winner of the winners' bracket in the finals. Should the winner of the losers' bracket win that match, then both will have lost only one match and one more match must be played to decide the champion. Should the winner of the winners' bracket win the first game, the tournament is over.

When you set up a double elimination tournament, the upper and lower ladders for the given number of players should be drawn first. Schedule the finals first and work backward, starting with the losers' bracket before proceeding to those matches in the upper bracket which have not yet been scheduled. If you do this correctly, the first matches will all be upper-bracket matches and there will be no need for losers of the first matches to play again until later in the tournament.

Example of a Double Elimination Tournament Ladder

1. For 8 sides (singles or doubles), A through H on ladder, if only one court is available for the tournament. Fourteen or 15 1½-hour matches can be played over a three-day period.

2. If two courts are available, the tournament can be condensed into two days and the time limit for each match can be extended up to two hours. In this event matches 1 through 6, 8 and 9, would be played on Saturday. Matches 10 and 11 would be played at 9:00 A.M. Sunday, matches 7 and 12 at 11:30 and the semi-finals as shown.

NOTE: Examples of ladders for odd numbers of entries including distribution of seeding and byes are available from the USCA office in New York City (see Appendices).

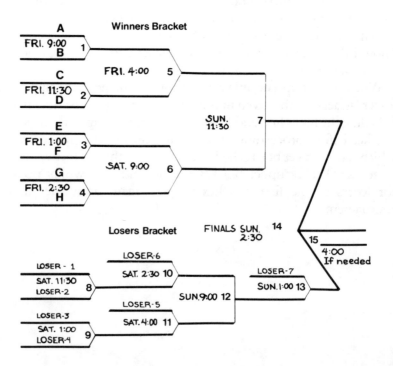

Bisques

The United States Croquet Association, like its British counterpart, uses a handicapping system of bisques to equalize match play between players or teams with different levels of skill. The USCA bisque rules allow a player to replay any given shot. The British Association bisque rule provides an additional continuation shot at the end of any stroke in the turn. The bisque is mostly used to correct an error and continue play; however, in the USCA game it may be used to attempt a different and more rewarding shot. Previously the USCA rules did not permit a player to use a bisque after a fault or to use more than one bisque a turn. Recently, it has been determined that these restrictions limit the effectiveness of the bisque. They have therefore been removed.

As is done in England and other countries, the United States is moving toward the establishment of a ranking system of its members, using bisques to designate individual play levels.

Bisques in Handicap Tournament Play

A handicap tournament provides for players of different caliber to compete reasonably equally. Naturally the best players in the tournament will receive few if any bisques and players of less skill will be awarded more. Depending upon the difference between skill levels of players within a tournament or club, bisques may range from zero to ten. Generally, the best player of a club or tournament should receive no bisques and is called a "scratch" player. The bisqueing of players should be based on singles play. However, quite often no proper comparisons between the best and worst players exist and players should be awarded bisques by the tournament committee based upon their general level of play.

When a tournament is broken down into flights according to skill level, usually the bisque differential is not greater than four or five. Quite often the players may play "net" bisques by subtracting the number of the best player's bisques from the number of bisques the higher handicap players have. This results in fewer bisques for each player with the best player playing at "scratch." "Full" bisques refers to matches played where all players are entitled to all designated bisques rather than playing off the lowest handicap.

Occasionally a tournament may be held where the teams are given bisques rather than the individual players. In this event, either player of a team may use the bisques and the teams may play at full or net bisques in accordance with the tournament rules.

Player Rankings and Handicaps

Eventually all USCA members will be ranked by a Grand Prix point system in which points will be awarded to every member based on their showing in local, invitational, regional and national tournaments. Once this system is established, a national ranking of players and a handicap allocation of bisques will be instituted. While determination of handicap within a USCA club is still best decided by that club's handicapping committee, our hope is that we will soon achieve a system compatible throughout the United States.

12

THE LUST FOR LAWNS

There can be little doubt that the better the lawn you have to play on, the faster your croquet skills will develop. It's unlikely, however, that most of the readers of this book have ever seen, let alone played on, a really good croquet lawn. Many more will have played on garden or backyard grass that was probably not flat and most certainly was uneven or bumpy. Simply put, the ideal lawn for first-class croquet will be as flat and smooth as possible because such a lawn reduces the element of chance and allows you to play a more advanced game with exacting shots and sophisticated tactics.

Unlike the British Isles, where climate and soil conditons are reasonably constant throughout, American conditions vary broadly. To attempt to provide a comprehensive treatise on the proper grass type or care and feeding of lawns from Alaska to Florida would fill several books.

Do not despair, however, for even those of you who think your lawns are beyond hope may find some helpful hints below. Existing backyard lawns with rolling or sloping areas dotted with trees can, with a little care, be great fun to play on.

Your most important concern should be the length of the grass. If it is too long, it will cause you to "force" your shots, with an inevitable toll of accuracy. Long grass will simply not allow you to attempt, let alone master, many of the roll or split shots. When you are forced to smash every ball, there is a tendency to hit down and cause the ball to jump as if it had hit a bump. Your first step in improving your lawn, then, is to cut it so the grass is as short as possible.

Your next concern should be the smoothness or texture of the lawn. Surprisingly enough, an even-textured greensward can be achieved even with lawns plagued by crabgrass, clover, daisies and plantains. Surely you want these reduced as much as possible; by using selective weed killers and weeding tools along with proper mowing, you can improve the texture. And by combining rolling and close-cutting, you can provide a harder or firmer surface. If you take care not to set the roller blades so low as to cut off the top turf, close-cutting can help control the weeds while providing a trimmer, faster surface.

As for leveling an existing irregular lawn, it may take a few years to achieve an excellent lawn. You will need to be adept at top-dressing with sifted soil and seed, filling and rolling back the turf, and removing some subsoil and relaying the turf. For smaller high spots, a hollow-tined fork will enable you to remove soil from beneath without disturbing the grass. These and other steps that may be recommended by your neighborhood garden center will all lead to a better-quality croquet court.

If you're contemplating the installation of a new court, we urge you to talk first with the golf course superintendent or greenskeeper of a local country club to determine the type of drainage and grass he uses for his putting greens.

Until contractors familiar with the installation of croquet courts become available, you might also check with a tennis court builder to discuss appropriate methods of leveling the area to be used.

Of the two basic methods of putting in grass—seeding or sodding—seeding, although less expensive, takes longer to become playable. Sodding is often faster, but the cost is higher. In either case, other factors to be considered are the watering systems for proper irrigation and drainage.

Ideally, a peripheral sprinkler system should be put in to avoid sprinkler heads on the court itself. Reasonable drainage can be achieved by a layer of gravel a few inches thick 5 to 6 inches under the top soil.

Three of the finest seeded croquet court installations we know are to be found at the Palm Beach Polo and Country Club in West Palm Beach, Florida, the Bon Vivant Country Club, Bourbonnais, Illinois, and the prestigious Meadow Club of Southampton, Long Island. The last, with 38 tennis courts, is now the largest lawn tennis club in the world. Eight of their newest tennis and their two croquet courts were installed with identical playing surfaces. Club ground superintendent Anthony Olender provides these suggestions:

> After the ground is properly leveled, it should be raked, limed and fertilized. Once the ground is ready, seed with a creeping bentgrass at a rate of 3–4 lbs. per 1,000 sq. feet. Overseeding is recommended for the next two years. Creeping bentgrass provides unsurpassed playing surface.
>
> However, if the selected site has a good, desirable grass, such as blue or fescue, already established, it can be overseeded with bentgrass. This would permit playing the following year.
>
> Follow-up care is essential, therefore you should consider the following:
> 1) Installing an irrigation system.
> 2) Purchasing a small lawnmower suitable for greens, preferably a Jacobsen.
>   a) set the cutting height of about 5/16" or 1/4".
>   b) court should be mowed at least three times a week.
> 3) Program of regular fertilizing, controlling weeds, crabgrass, fungus and insects.

In sharp contrast with the two- or three-year lawn development program above was the three-month installation at the Palm Beach Polo and Country Club in 1980. Faced with providing playable lawns for the USCA's National Club Team Championship matches the first of April, ground was broken in mid-January; plastic drainage pipes were laid in 20 inches of gravel, 12 to 18 inches of topsoil was graded, leveled, sprigged with a mixture of winter rye and Bermuda Number 327 and rolled off. A sprinkler system arranged for complete coverage without interfering in the flat court area was installed in an 8-foot-wide observation area 12 inches above the playing area surrounding the two full-size courts. A tent pavilion and four shade awnings along with some attractive landscaping were the finishing touches for what has been praised by Americans and internationals alike as one of the finest croquet facilities in the world.

Credit for this remarkable installation must go to the late Paul Butler, a Palm Beach Polo and Country Club director better known as "Mr. Polo" and the creator of Butler National Golf Course in Oak

Brook, Illinois. In his late eighties, Butler took to croquet with great enthusiasm. His day-to-day attention to every aspect of the court's development ensured its successful completion in what has to be record time.

These beautiful lawns have matured since Paul's death and serve today as the headquarter courts and principal teaching facility of the USCA in Florida.

Sodding, or the laying down of already growing turf on a preleveled court site, has also proved successful at several USCA member clubs. By calling in a talented neighboring golf course superintendent to supervise its installation, the Beach Club of Palm Beach had two tournament quality lawns in play within two months of putting down the sod. And at the Pinehurst Hotel and Country Club in North Carolina, in what must be considered the most ambitious croquet installations to date, three full-size courts were carved out of a sloping hillside in front of the golf clubhouse, sodded with putting green grass in June of 1982, and were ready for the Southern Regional USCA Championship play in late August. These three beautiful tiered greenswards at the country's leading golf complex, together with one court poolside at the nearby hotel, give Pinehurst the distinction of being the first site in America with four international quality croquet courts. Of historical note is the fact that the first sport facility installed by James Tufts, who created Pinehurst in 1895, was a croquet court.

Whether starting a croquet court from scratch or improving an existing lawn, a program of continuing maintenance is a must. For that reason golf, tennis and other clubs that have the equipment and staff to care for the courts properly are ideally suited as sites for croquet clubs.

Similarly, residential resorts and retirement communities are able to establish and maintain excellent facilities. Colleges and schools often have lawn areas that can be utilized effectively, and, with encouragement from interested faculty and alumni, can even be improved to first-class level.

Another opportunity for establishing courts rests in the parks and recreational departments of towns and cities. If properly approached, these agencies can be convinced of the healthful, social and beautification benefits of croquet facilities.

In New York City, Beverly Hills and San Francisco, for example, local clubs are playing on lawns originally set down as lawn bowling greens. The New York Croquet Club shares a lawn with the New York Lawn Bowling Club, an arrangement that has worked well for more than ten years. These lawns have served as the site for the first six USCA National Singles and Doubles Croquet Championships.

As a result of the media coverage of the Nationals, a number of other USCA clubs, in approaching their local authorities, have suggested that with any new installation their parks department might consider one which could serve both croquet and lawn bowling to maximize the use of the facility. The principal concern of players of both sports is ensuring the smooth surface of the lawns; this can be achieved by properly plugging the holes created by the wickets when the bowlers are to use the lawn. (What follows is also applicable to lawn tennis courts, which are frequently used as croquet lawns.) Styrofoam carrot-shaped plugs should be inserted in the wicket holes and sprinkled with grass clippings or topped with half-inch-deep grass plugs. Avoid filling the holes with soil, which will ultimately cause a mound to develop under the wicket.

While we're on that subject, ruts may be worn between the uprights with constant play and wickets should be rotated from time to time. To do this, simply remove the wicket and reset it with one upright in the existing hole and the other in a new one to the side. Make certain that all wickets are kept in line with one another by rotating them in the same direction. Then fill the remaining old holes with grass clippings; during dry weather, these holes should be repacked in a day or so, as the clippings will shrink.

The USCA greens committee, under the direction of The Bon Vivant Country Club (Bourbonnais, Illinois) golf course superintendent J. Michael Hart is accumulating a great deal of information on the subject of court installation and care and will make it available to member clubs in the near future.

13

CLUBS

Of the original five charter USCA clubs—the Westhampton Mallet Club, the New York Croquet Club, the Palm Beach Croquet Club, the Croquet Club of Bermuda, and the Green Gables Croquet Club of Spring Lake, New Jersey—no two are truly alike. Let's look at the basic types of croquet clubs which make up the Association today.

1) *Family-sized clubs* are home-based groups with a one-or-two-family core. Neighboring or other family members are added as their interest is raised. Play is centered on primarily one or two backyard courts, which tend to be improved by the land owner as the playing level increases. These clubs, which represent 20 percent of the Association membership, enjoy the game for the opportunity to compete among themselves. Family fun is the key ingredient.

2) *Private croquet clubs* represent an expanded, organized group of from 10 to 100 members where croquet makes up either a substantial part or the whole of the club's sports activities. They are composed mainly of adults who enjoy the competitive challenge of the game as well as the broader social aspects. These clubs often establish more formal croquet facilities, with only one or perhaps many courts, and share the cost of proper equipment and maintenance. In some instances they utilize a single member's or several members' home courts, or arrange to play on semi-public or public grounds. All five USCA charter members are in

Elephant's Walk, Bermuda, built by US Croquet Hall of Famer Duncan McMartin. The Finals of the annual Croquet Club of Bermuda Invitational are held here.

Croquet at the historical center court of the Newport Casino, home of the Newport Croquet Club, just adjacent to the Tennis Hall of Fame.

this group, with New York's 120 members making the NYCC the largest. Thirty percent of the Association clubs are in this category.

3) *Country, tennis and sports clubs* are primarily dominated by activities other than croquet, a game presented to their membership as an individual sports alternative. A croquet committee is formed to organize activities for those club members who are interested in the sport. Proceeds of guest fees can be used to fund equipment needs or social functions related to the croquet groups. The club encourages its croquet-playing members to join the USCA as individuals in order that they may enjoy its benefits. Among the USCA members in this category are the Meadow Club, Southampton, L.I., and the Beach Club, Palm Beach.

4) *Resorts, hotels and inns* are increasingly adding croquet to their roster of athletic activities, and this represents an exciting and positive trend for the sport. Facilities range in size from one small court at New England inns (such as the fourteen-room Pointway Inn in Edgartown on Martha's Vineyard) to the four new full-sized international-level courts at Pinehurst in North Carolina.

These installations provide numerous esthetic, social, recreational and promotional benefits, including an attractive and functional use of open space and an added sports and social activity for guests and local residents. At the Rancho Santa Fe Inn in California, for example, the courts are used as the site for a local private USCA club. These resorts, hotels and inns (along with the country and sports clubs) account for 30 percent of the USCA membership today and benefit from the ongoing publicity that surrounds their croquet tournaments and events.

In addition, if these resorts and hotels have a sufficient number of adequate-sized, well-maintained courts, they may serve as sites for USCA teaching clinics/schools.

5) *Schools, colleges and universities.* The fast-growing USCA College Division was launched in November 1980 with the Harvard and Yale Croquet clubs' first competitive match. In March of 1982 the first USCA National Intercollegiate Croquet Championships attracted Harvard, Yale, Vassar, Brown, Brandeis, Columbia, the University of Virginia, the University of Florida and the University of Southern Cali-

fornia teams to Palm Beach, Florida. As has been proven at Oxford and Cambridge in England, future national champions will undoubtedly come from intraschool tournaments (fraternities, sororities, etc.), and interschool state, regional and national competitions.

6) *Retirement groups and communities* are another contingent that is expressing mounting interest. Croquet offers a great deal of enjoyment and satisfaction as a healthful competitive outlet for those unable to participate in more physically demanding outdoor sports.

Member clubs pay annual dues to the USCA ranging from $100 for family membership, $150 for private country, tennis and sports clubs and small resorts, to $250 for hotels and larger resorts. Additional individual members of these clubs pay $15 per person or $20 a couple annually for USCA membership cards, which entitle them to play in USCA–sanctioned tournaments and provides playing privileges to other USCA clubs (subject to each member club's guest rules). Also, private club invitational tournaments may be sanctioned by the USCA but limited to the invitees of the sponsoring host club.

The USCA provides all member clubs with a number of benefits, including organizational assistance for croquet activities. Also available to clubs and USCA members are educational clinics and tournament formats, individual subscriptions to the *U.S. Croquet Gazette,* and discounts on croquet equipment and instructional material. These savings more than offset the annual dues the club pays.

For additional information on club formation and membership, contact the United States Croquet Association, 635 Madison Avenue, New York, New York 10022 or call (212) 688-5495.

14

UNITED STATES CROQUET ASSOCIATION RULES

(With a Note on British and American Rules)

Since their adoption in 1976, the USCA Rules for both the 6-wicket, 1-stake and the 9-wicket, 2-stake games have undergone evolutionary changes. First published in the book *Croquet, the Complete Guide to History, Strategy, Rules and Records,* by Jim Charlton and William Thompson (Scribner's, 1977), they were updated in the *U.S. Croquet Gazette* in 1980 and 1981 and in the 1982 USCA Rule Book.

As with the English Laws of Croquet, which have been repeatedly redrafted over the past century, the USCA rules will continue to evolve and incorporate changes that clarify and update the intentions of the Rules Committee.

To those readers of this book who possess any of these earlier versions, we urge you to study the following newly revised rules with particular attention to the shift to the Standard Rules of those previously in the Advanced Rules section.

The most important of these rule shifts involves the *croquet stroke* (from Advanced Rule 2 to Rule 25 in the Standard Rules), which now requires the striker's ball to be placed in contact with the roqueted ball instead of a mallet head away.

After carefully watching the dramatic improvement of those club players who have followed our encouragement and have played this rule for the past several years, it was felt important and timely to make the shift now to enable all the new players coming to the game to start building the shot-making skills this rule ensures.

Other significant changes to the Standard Rules include the prohibition of the push, pull, crush, double-tapping and foot shots. That only a rover may stake out another rover has been standard since 1980.

Bisques may now be taken even if a fault has been committed, and more than one may be taken in a single turn (Rules 29 and 30).

Each time a player passes through the one-back wicket, his opponent may remove any existing deadness from one of his balls (Rule 37a).

There are many more minor changes that have been incorporated in these revised rules and we urge you to study them all.

The body of the USCA rules consists of sections as follows:

Section I—The Court and Setting, Equipment and Accessories
Section II—The Object of the Game
Section III—Customs and Etiquette
Section IV—Rules of the Standard American 6-Wicket Game and Advanced Game

The 6-Wicket Game

I.
The Court and Setting, Equipment and Accessories

THE STANDARD COURT

The standard court is a rectangle, measuring 35 by 28 yards [105 by 84 feet]. Its boundaries shall be marked out clearly, the INSIDE edge of the definitive border being the actual boundary. Nylon string (1/16 inch) stapled or otherwise affixed to the ground can be used for the boundary lines.

COURT REFERENCES

The four corners of the court are known respectively as Corners 1, 2, 3, and 4. The four boundaries are known as South, West, North and East boundaries—regardless of the orientation of the court.

THE STANDARD SETTING

The stake shall be set in the center of the court. The wickets shall be set parallel to the North and South boundaries; the centers of the two inner wickets 21 feet to the north and south of the stake; the centers of the four outer wickets 21 feet from their adjacent boundaries. This is the preferred court size and setting for major tournaments.

MODIFIED COURT SIZE AND SETTING

Should the area be too small to accommodate a standard court, a modified court may be laid out in accordance with the above by maintaining the same proportions of five length units long by four

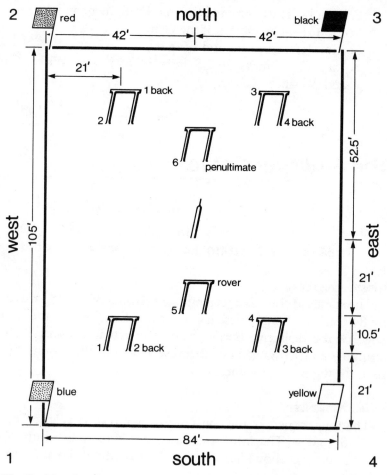

The 6-wicket, 1-stake court.

length units wide or by using a smaller modified length unit. EXAMPLE: Units of ten feet could be used to set the court dimensions. Thus 40 feet wide by 50 feet long with the stake in the middle at the intersection of the two diagonals is a possible setup. The corner wickets are 1 unit (10 feet) from their adjacent boundaries. The center wickets are 1 unit (10 feet) in each direction from the stake. Local conditions may require other layouts, but the size above is generally considered the minimum for this game.

EQUIPMENT

WICKETS

The wickets shall be of round iron $5/8$ inch diameter and of uniform thickness. They shall be 12 inches in height above the ground measured to the crown of the wicket, vertical and firmly fixed. The crown shall be straight and at right angles to the uprights, which shall not be less than $3^{11}/16$ inches nor more than 4 inches apart uniformly between the uprights (inside measurement) provided that all wickets on any one court shall be of the same dimensions. The wickets shall be painted white, the crown of the first wicket colored blue, and that of the last wicket which is known as the rover wicket, red. (This style of wicket is used in major tournaments.)

Another form of light-weight iron wicket (sometimes referred to as a "winter wicket" since it can be set into hard ground more easily) is $7/16$ inch in diameter with 4 inches between uprights. It is used in non-tournament games where circumstances warrant.

THE STAKE

The stake shall be of wood, of a uniform diameter above the ground of $1^1/2$ inches. It shall be 18 inches in height above the ground, exclusive of a detachable portion to hold clips, vertical and firmly fixed. The base shall be painted white with blue, red, black, and yellow bands descending in that order from the top.

THE BALLS

The balls shall be colored respectively blue, red, black, and yellow. They shall be $3^5/8$ inches in diameter and of even weight, not less than $15^3/4$ ounces nor more than $16^1/4$ ounces. Faulty or damaged balls may be changed during play.

MALLETS

The head of the mallet shall be of wood, or any other material, provided that the player shall gain no advantage over wood. Metal may be used for weighting or strengthening it. The two faces shall be parallel, perpendicular and identical in every respect. There may be a bevelled edge which shall not be considered as part of the face. A player may not change his mallet during a turn except in the case of damage affecting use.

ACCESSORIES

The following accessories should be supplied for guidance, convenience and decoration. The accessories do not form part of the setting of the court. Accordingly, any such accessories impeding a striker may be temporarily removed.

CORNER FLAGS

Flags colored blue, red, black and yellow shall be placed on corners 1, 2, 3 and 4 respectively. The flags shall be mounted on pegs about one foot high. The pegs shall be touching the boundary but no part shall be on the court. These are used primarily as an aid in judging distances and are not essential to the game.

EXTENSION TO FINISHING STAKE

A detachable portion to hold clips shall be attached to the top of the stake.

CLIPS

The function of clips is to indicate the state of the game on the court. The wicket or stake next in order for every ball at the beginning of every turn shall be distinguished by a clip of color corresponding with that of the ball. When a ball scores a wicket, the striker shall remove the clip and, at the end of the turn, place it upon the appropriate wicket or stake. When the stake is scored, the clip shall be removed from the court. The first six wickets shall be distinguished by placing the clip on the crown of the wicket, the last six by placing it on one of the uprights. Each player and/or referee should call the attention of the other to a misplaced clip as soon as the mistake is observed, and the clip should then be properly placed.

It is also permissible and desirable that a check-fence just high enough to arrest the progress of balls be placed round the outside of the court about a yard from the boundary.

DEADNESS BOARD

In order to help the contestants (and spectators) to remember what balls they are dead on, it is useful to have a white board approximately a yard square with the four ball colors permanently affixed in proper sequence either horizontally along the top or vertically on the left side and 12 colored discs (three each of the four ball colors) to be hung on nails or hinged wooden markers and able to be flipped up and down. These are arranged in four columns (one column per ball) so that they may be exposed as each ball's deadness occurs and removed from view when the ball's deadness ends.

II.
The Object of the Game

SINGLES

The singles game is played between two players—one of whom plays the blue and black, the other the red and yellow balls. The object of the game is for a player to make both of his balls score the 12 wicket points and the stake point, a total of 26 points, before his adversary.

DOUBLES

The doubles game is played between two sides, each side consisting of two players. One team plays the blue and black balls and the other the red and yellow balls. Each player plays the same ball throughout the game. As in singles, the object is to have one team score the total of 26 points before its adversaries.

IN BOTH GAMES

A ball scores a wicket point by passing through the wicket in the order and in the direction shown in illustration. This is known as running a wicket. But a ball which has first hit another ball (roqueted) cannot thereafter in the same stroke score a point for itself, except at the first wicket as in Rule 9. A ball which has scored all 12 wicket points is known as a rover. It can then score the stake by hitting it. In time limit tournament games, wicket (and stake) points are added at the end of the game and the team with the most points is the winner.

HOW PLAY IS MADE

Play is made by striking a ball with a mallet. The player so playing is called the striker, and the ball that he strikes, the striker's ball. The striker may never strike an adversary's ball with his mallet. By striking his own ball the striker may cause any other ball to move and/or to score a point.

THE TURN

The players play each turn in sequence (blue, red, black and yellow). A player is initially entitled to one stroke in a turn, after which his turn ends unless in that stroke his striker's ball has scored a wicket point or hit another ball. When the wicket is scored, the striker is entitled to play one additional or continuation stroke (EXCEPTION: Rule 51). When another ball (whether opponent's or partner's) is hit, the striker is said to have made a "roquet" on that ball and he becomes "dead" on that ball and is entitled to two extra strokes.

The first of these two strokes is known as the "croquet" stroke, and is made after moving and placing the striker's ball in contact with the roqueted ball.

If, in the croquet stroke, the croqueted ball is sent off the court or the striker's ball is sent off the court without first having made another roquet, the turn ends. During his turn a striker may roquet each ball he is "alive" on once, and he may make a further roquet on each ball provided that since he has last roqueted, his striker's ball has scored a wicket point for itself and has thus cleared itself of its "deadness." Thus, by a series of strokes entitling him to continue, the striker may make one or more points during one turn. Such a series is known as "making a break." But continuation strokes are not cumulative so that the striker who:

a) first scores a wicket and hits another ball in the same stroke may either take one additional (continuation) stroke and not be dead on the ball so hit, or roquet the ball and take two;

b) makes a roquet in a croquet stroke immediately takes croquet and continues accordingly;

c) scores a wicket for his striker's ball in a croquet stroke plays only one continuation stroke.

BALL IN HAND

A ball in hand is any ball which has to be moved, and is therefore lifted and given a fresh position on the court in accordance with the Rules, i.e.:

a) a ball which has made a roquet;
b) a ball off the court;
c) a ball lifted under Rule 13 or Advanced Rule 1;
d) a ball which has to be repositioned after a fault or irregularity.

BALL OFF THE COURT

A ball off the court is a ball in hand as soon as it goes off the court or when its vertical axis crosses the boundary line (more than halfway over).

REPLACEMENT OF BALLS OFF THE COURT
AND NEAR BOUNDARIES

After each stroke all balls off the court shall be replaced one mallet head in from the point where they went out. After each stroke all balls within 9 inches of the boundary line except the striker's shall be replaced a mallet head in from the line.

III.
Customs and Etiquette

The following, while not including specific rules or penalty related action, should be considered important and helpful to the conduct and enjoyment of the game.

PRESENCE ON COURT

A player should not remain on the court in line of sight or area of visibility while his adversary is playing, or move onto it until it is clear that he has finished or may be about to make a questionable stroke.

EXPEDITION OF PLAY

A player should play his strokes as quickly as possible, and in doubles should avoid wasting time in prolonged discussion with his partner. (More than 75 seconds is considered excessive.)

SPECTATORS

Spectators should abstain from audible comments on the game; from offering advice to players during a game; and from calling attention to any error committed or about to be committed by any player. A spectator may reply to a question by a player on a point of fact with the consent of his adversary. A player should not take advantage of any error or omission unnoticed by himself or his partner to which his attention has been drawn during the game by the comments or attitude of the spectators.

ADVICE AND AIDS

No player is entitled to advice from anyone other than his partner in doubles. It must be a matter of conscience how a player acts when in receipt of unsolicited information or advice. Warning a player other than his partner that he is about to run a wrong wicket or play with the wrong ball constitutes advice, and in tournaments players and spectators must not so warn.

A mark shall not be made, either inside or outside the court, for the purpose of guiding the striker in the direction or strength of a stroke. A partner may use his mallet to indicate a spot, but it must be removed before the stroke.

QUESTIONABLE STROKE

A player about to play a stroke, of which either the fairness or the effect (i.e., possible foul or when aiming at a ball in our near a wicket) may be doubtful, should himself suggest to his adversary that a referee be called to watch the stroke. The striker or opponent should signal for a referee or umpire by holding his mallet vertically above his head.

WHEN THE PLAYERS' OPINIONS DIFFER

If a ball has to be replaced because of the carelessness of a player, the offending party should ordinarily defer to the opinion of the other. When the question is whether a roquet has been made on a ball or whether the ball has moved, the positive opinion is generally to be preferred to the negative opinion. If there are any reliable witnesses, the players should agree to consult them in order to solve the differences; but no player should consult a witness without the expressed permission of the other player.

TESTING THE POSITION OF A BALL

The striker should not test whether a ball has run a wicket by placing his mallet against the wicket without first consulting his opponent. Any such test should be made in conjunction with the opponent, or, if either party so desires, by a referee or independent person if available. The same principle applies when the question is whether a ball is out of bounds, or may be lifted, moved, or wiped, if the position of replacement is critical. All such decisions made between strokes should be made jointly.

WHEN CALLING A REFEREE

In tournaments, a referee should always be called before a questionable stroke, and all disputes should be referred to a referee. If the opponent fails to call a referee before what he should have realized to be a questionable stroke, he should not appeal. He should confine himself to requesting the striker to take the initiative in calling for a referee if another such stroke is to be played. But it may be that the adversary is of the opinion that the striker is making faults such as "pushing" or "double tapping" in an unhampered stroke; if so, he should inform the striker with a view to a referee being called to watch a stroke.

Should any player feel that an opponent is making repeated faults (and the referee concurs), such as failing to move or shake the roqueted ball in his croquet stroke, he may request that a referee watch all such subsequent shots but must inform that opponent of that request. The referee or an appointed umpire may, at the request of either side, watch for faults under Rule 25 e & f, and under this circumstance such a referee or umpire's decision shall prevail.

UMPIRES

An umpire is any person appointed by a referee of that tournament to act with the following limited powers:

a) As a referee to judge whether a ball hits another ball, moves or shakes in the croquet stroke or whether a ball hits the stake (peg).
b) As a referee to judge whether a ball has completed the running of a hoop or is on or off the court.
c) As a referee to judge any questionable stroke.

IV.
The Rules of the Standard American 6-Wicket Game and Advanced Game

PART 1. Use of the Mallet

1. A player must hit the ball with either striking end of his mallet head. He may hold any part of his mallet-shaft with one or both hands, and may use any stance he wishes so long as he does not rest his hand, arm or shaft of the mallet on the ground.

2. a) In a single-ball stroke the striker may not push or pull his ball. NOTE: In above a "push" or "pull" means maintaining contact between mallet and ball for an appreciable period or any acceleration following a check of the mallet head after its initial contact with the ball. Nor may he;

b) Strike his ball audibly or distinctly twice in the same stroke (double tap) or maintain contact between mallet and ball after his ball has hit another ball, except that no fault can be commited under this rule if the cause of the second hit or the maintenance of contact is due to the making of a roquet or to interference by a ball hitting or bouncing from a wicket or stake in that stroke.

3. It shall be counted a stroke if in the course of striking his ball a player's mallet hits a wicket but not the ball, or if he drives his mallet into the ground without contacting the ball; or misses it entirely.

4. a) If a ball lies so that a player cannot strike it squarely, he may not place another mallet against the ball and hit that mallet with his own.

b) The striker may not move or shake a ball at rest by hitting a wicket or stake with the mallet. Nor may he;

c) Strike his ball so as to cause it to touch an upright or the stake while still in contact with the mallet (crush shot). Nor may he;

d) Strike his ball when lying in contact with an upright or the stake other than in the direction away from the upright or the stake (crush shot).

5. In the course of the stroke the player may strike only his own ball without touching another ball with his mallet.

The penalty for committing a fault under Rules 1, 2, 4 and 5 is end of turn and all balls replaced.

PART 2. Starting the Game and Wicket #1

6. The toss of a coin determines the starting order of play. The side winning the toss has the choice of playing first and third with blue and black or second and fourth with red and yellow.

7. All balls must start from the starting tee in the order shown on the stake (blue, red, black, yellow) and must continue in that order throughout the game, or until put out of play. The starting tee must be marked one mallet's length before the first wicket by two coins or markers one mallet's head apart. The ball must be played from between these two markers.

8. Each ball is dead until it has made wicket #1 (the blue crown wicket).

9. A player who has not make wicket #1 may drive his ball and hit any other ball which has likewise not made that wicket, so as to put it into position, out of position, or through the wicket. This ends his turn unless his ball also makes a clear passage through the wicket, which entitles his ball to one additional stroke. The other ball which has thus been put through the wicket shall be considered to have made the wicket but is not entitled to an extra stroke.

10. A player who drives or caroms through wicket #1 is deemed to have made the wicket, and is entitled to one extra stroke, but is nevertheless dead on all balls which have not made this wicket.

11. A player who drives or caroms through wicket #1 and in the same stroke strikes a ball which is not itself through that wicket is not penalized; he is entitled to one additional stroke, and the other ball is replaced.

12. Any ball which has made the first wicket may not directly impede the stroke or alter the position of any other ball which has not made the first wicket and may be lifted and replaced after the stroke of the ball in play. EXCEPTION: Rule 13b.

13. A player who has made wicket #1 may hit only those balls on which he is alive. A ball which has not made wicket #1 and which lies in the intended path of any ball which is through that wicket may a) be lifted and replaced after the stroke of the ball in play (i.e., a ball for wicket #2 back may lift and after his stroke replace the one which has not made #1) or

b) it may be cannoned (peeled) in either direction (back or into the game) by a second or third ball (see Rule 37).

PART 3. Making a Wicket

14. To score a wicket point, a ball must make a complete passage through a wicket and in the proper direction, and is considered through the wicket if the mallet-head, when placed against the approach side of the wicket, does not touch the ball.

15. A ball stopping in the wicket, or one which goes through but rolls back into it, has not made the wicket.

16. If a ball is for a wicket but on the wrong side, it may be played through the wicket to the approach side, but it must clear the wicket on the non-playing approach side in order to be played through subsequently.

17. A ball which is dead on another ball lying at or partially in the approach to the wicket (except prior to wicket #1), may not hit that ball in trying to make the wicket. If it does, the wicket is not made and the player's turn ends, with his ball and the ball so hit being replaced. However, a player may use the jump shot to make a blocked wicket, a blocked stake, or at any time.

18. A ball which is dead on another ball lying beyond (not intruding into) a wicket must make a complete passage through the wicket, either before or after contact, if any, to be alive and receive one extra stroke.

19. A ball running a wicket other than the one in the proper sequence or direction shall not receive credit for that wicket nor receive an extra stroke, except if it is a rover. See Part 8 Rule 41.

20. A player may block (stymie) a wicket twice with a ball upon which the opponent is dead, but on the opponent's third turn he must leave the wicket clear or be lifted and replaced after that turn. A ball which is encroaching on the direct path through a wicket is considered to be a block or stymie.

21. Upon making his first wicket of a turn, a player should remove his clip, and at the end of his turn attach it to his next wicket. For the first six wickets the clip is placed on the crown, thereafter on the uprights. Each player, referee or official scorer should call attention to a misplaced clip, which should then be properly placed.

PART 4. Wicket Points, Roquet, Croquet and Additional Strokes

22. Wicket Points: a) When the striker's ball has scored a wicket point the striker shall be entitled to play one continuation stroke in any direction. If the striker's ball or any other ball it hits on that

stroke goes out of bounds, his turn would end with any ball off the court replaced one mallet's head in from where it went out.

b) When a ball other than the striker's is caused to score a wicket point, it is said to have been peeled through that wicket but does not receive a continuation stroke.

23. Roquet: a) During a turn the striker is entitled to hit (roquet) each ball he is alive on and thereby earn two additional strokes. (EXCEPTION: Rule 51.) He may further roquet on each ball provided he clears his deadness by scoring another wicket point for his ball.

b) The striker makes a roquet when his ball hits one it is not dead on either directly or by glancing off a wicket or stake.

c) When hitting two or more balls upon which he is alive in the same stroke, the roquet will be deemed to have been made on the first ball it hit with the latter ball being replaced, or if hit simultaneously, the one to be nominated by the striker as the roqueted ball.

d) A ball which has made a roquet cannot thereafter in the same stroke make or score a wicket point for itself.

24. A striker who makes his wicket and hits (roquets) another ball on the same stroke must hit it again in order to earn two additional strokes. Unless he has driven either ball off the court in that same stroke, the striker may elect to take one continuation stroke and shall not be considered dead on the ball so hit. The hit ball is not replaced.

25. The Croquet Stroke: a) When a roquet is made, the striker's ball becomes a ball in hand and is brought to the roqueted ball.

b) To take croquet, the striker places his ball in contact with the roqueted ball however he chooses, but it may not be touching any other ball.

c) Before playing his stroke, the striker may touch or steady the roqueted ball and may further apply such pressure by hand or foot, but not by mallet, as is reasonably necessary to make it hold its position. He may not move any ball intentionally, but if he does so unintentionally he may replace it without penalty.

d) The ball hitherto known as the roqueted ball is in the croquet stroke known as the croqueted ball.

e) The striker now makes the croquet stroke with the balls placed as in (b) above and in doing so must move or shake the croqueted ball.

f) Should an opponent question the striker as to whether he has seen the croqueted ball move or shake, the striker must reply in the affirmative or negative (yes or no). The striker may only confirm that he has seen or not seen the ball move so that if he is uncertain the ball will have been deemed not to have moved.

> PENALTY: Unless the fault is condoned, the striker's turn ends and all balls remain where they lie at the end of the stroke (EXCEPTION: Rule 50) with no wicket or stake points scored and any other ball hit in this stroke replaced.

g) After the croquet stroke, the striker shall be entitled to play an additional stroke unless his turn has ended under Rule 51 or has made another legal croquet, whereafter he would take croquet from that ball.

h) The striker may not place his foot or hand on his ball during the croquet stroke.

i) After each stroke any ball, except the striker's, less than a mallet's head off the boundary is replaced that length from the line. If that ball cannot be replaced directly in from the line from where it rests due to the presence of another ball, it may at the discretion of the striker be placed one mallet's head in from the line and up to a mallet's head in either direction from, but not in contact with, the ball.

26. Any player may handle any ball which is replaceable after contact, or may return any ball which has made a roquet to its player without penalty. A player may place a ball for his partner's croquet stroke to save time, and may give a temporary mark which must be removed before the stroke is taken. A player may lift his ball to clean it at any time during the game, but must advise his opponent before doing so. Any ball accidentally moved shall be replaced without penalty. EXCEPTION: Rule 56a.

PART 5. Bisques

27. A bisque is a handicap stroke wherein the striker is allowed to replay a shot from its original position on the court. A bisque may be taken only if the ball can be replaced accurately, by having marked the ball with a coin (directly behind the ball) or a mallet head from the boundary line. The intention of taking a bisque need not be announced before the original shot is made.

28. A bisque may be taken for only the immediately preceding stroke.

29. A bisque may be taken if the original shot resulted in a

penalty; for example: out-of-bounds, hitting a dead ball, or striking the wrong ball.

30. A player may take more than one bisque per turn.

31. In doubles tournaments the players will individually play with their full quota of bisques (i.e., a 2 handicap receives two bisques for his ball only).

32. In singles tournaments a player plays only his handicap quota for both balls (i.e., 2 handicap receives two bisques total, which can be used for either ball, or both taken on one ball).

PART 6. Dead Ball

33. When a striker's ball roquets another upon which it is alive, it is immediately dead on that ball until the player has made his next wicket in order, but he may play off it as in Rule 25. EXCEPTION: When the striker's ball roquets a ball out-of-bounds, his turn ends, but he remains alive on that ball, which is replaced one mallet's head from where it went out.

34. If a striker's ball directly hits a ball on which it is dead, the striker's turn ends and both balls shall be replaced. EXCEPTION: During a croquet stroke, the ball being croqueted may be hit by the striker's ball more than once without penalty (e.g.: twice during a split or trundle shot).

35. If a ball roquets one on which it is alive and therefore during the same stroke hits another ball, whether alive or dead on it, the latter shall be replaced without penalty (i.e. no penalty if out-of-bounds, or credit for wicket or stake). The player must play off the first ball hit and is not dead on the second ball if originally alive on it.

36. If during a croquet shot the player's ball strikes another ball upon which it is dead, the turn ends, and the ball just roqueted and the striker's ball are replaced with the croqueted ball remaining where it lies after the stroke and given credit for any wicket or stake point made. If, however, in a croquet shot, the player's ball strikes a ball on which it is alive, it has then made a roquet on that ball and must play off it as in Rule 25.

37. a) Any third or fourth ball struck (cannoned) by a roqueted or croqueted ball (whether alive or dead on it) will be treated as having been played directly, with all balls remaining where they lie at the end of the stroke. The struck ball is given credit for wicket or stake points if made and no deadness is credited between the roqueted or croqueted ball and the cannoned ball. If no fault has

occurred, the striker may then take his next stroke. If any ball (except the striker's on the roquet stroke) goes out of bounds, the striker's turn ends, all balls remain where they lie, and the out-of-bounds ball(s) is (are) replaced 9 inches in from the boundary where it went out.

b) Special relief from deadness: When each ball of both sides passes through the 1-back wicket, the opposing side may clear the deadness from one of its balls. The side receiving this relief must declare which ball it chooses to clear before playing the first shot of its next turn or no relief is given. The side whose ball has just made 1-back may request that the opposing side declare which ball they choose to clear, at which point that side must declare.

Should a striker peel his opponent through the 1-back hoop, the striker will have an option to clear either his or his partner's ball. If the peel is accomplished on the roquet stroke, the striker may clear himself but must place his ball in contact with the roqueted ball and play his croquet stroke, whereupon he is dead on the croqueted ball. If the peel is accomplished on the croquet shot, the striker may clear himself on all balls and play his continuation stroke as if he had just scored a wicket. A rover ball may be cleared of deadness when an opponent scores 1-back but may not clear himself of last deadness.

PART 7. Alive Ball

38. A ball becomes alive upon being driven through its proper wicket in the proper direction.

39. A ball driven through its wicket by a striker's ball on its roquet stroke which is: a) alive on it, shall be considered alive and through the wicket, but is not entitled to an extra stroke;

b) dead on it, is not considered to have made the wicket, and both balls are replaced.

PART 8. Rover and Finishing the Game

40. A player who has made all the wickets in the proper sequence becomes a rover and is considered alive on all balls upon making the #12 wicket (the red crown wicket).

41. To become alive from a 2- or a 3-ball deadness, a rover may go through any wicket in any direction, receiving an extra stroke. If the ball does not clear the wicket, it must, unless knocked out, continue through in the same direction in order to be considered clear.

42. a) A rover ball may hit any other ball once per turn. Before clearing himself he must be dead on at least two balls, but nevertheless he remains dead on the ball last hit before clearing, until he hits a different ball, whereupon his temporary deadness disappears.

b) A rover that runs a wicket in clearing its deadness and in the same stroke hits a ball upon which it was last dead incurs no penalty, and unless either ball is driven out of bounds, both balls remain where they lie and the striker is entitled to take his continuation stroke.

43. A rover's ball may only be driven into the stake (either on a roquet or croquet stroke) by another rover which is alive on it (EXCEPTION: Rule 35), whereupon it will be considered to have finished the game (and scored a point for itself), and shall be immediately removed from the court.

44. A rover ball roqueted into the stake by a striker's ball which is dead on it shall be replaced and considered still in play.

45. A rover ball hitting the stake after making a roquet is not staked out and shall play normally off the roqueted ball.

46. When one ball of a side has staked out of the game it is removed from the court immediately and play continues in the proper rotation with the staked out ball losing all subsequent turns.

47. If in a roquet shot a striker's rover ball drives another rover ball into the stake, it is removed from play and the striker receives two strokes taken a mallet's head in any direction from the stake.

48. The game is won by the side that finishes the game with both balls first, or in a time limit game by the side scoring the highest total of wicket or stake points.

PART 9. Faults and Penalties for Out-of-Bounds, Playing Out of Turn, Playing the Wrong Ball, Illegal Shots and Condoned Play

49. A ball is out-of-bounds when its vertical axis crosses the boundary line (more than halfway over). It shall be replaced one mallet head (nine inches) from where it went out, or, if near a corner, at least one mallet head from both boundary lines.

50. At the end of every stroke all balls except the striker's less than a mallet's head from the boundary are placed that length from the line. a) If the space to which such a ball should be placed be occupied by another ball, the replaced ball shall be put up to a mallet's head in either direction from the said ball at the discretion of the striker.

b) Should two balls be sent over the boundary or less than a mallet's head from the boundary at the same place, the ball first out of bounds or closest to it is placed first with the second placed as in (a) above.

51. If the striker sends any ball at any time out-of-bounds, his turn ends. EXCEPTION: If, during a roquet, the striker's ball either goes out or caroms into a third ball sending the latter out. (Also see Rule 33.)

52. If a ball is played out of turn, all balls are replaced as at the beginning of play, and the play is resumed in proper sequence with the offending ball losing its turn in that sequence.

53. If the striker plays a foot or hand shot his turn ends and both balls are replaced.

54. If an opponent observes the striker playing a stroke with any ball, except the striker's in his continuing or croquet stroke, not properly placed on the boundary line, he may request that the shot be replayed from the proper position providing he does so before the next stroke of the turn. If he does not so request the replay, the shot will be deemed condoned.

55. If a player plays the wrong ball, his turn ends and all balls are replaced where they were before the fault occurred. In a singles game, a striker playing the wrong partner ball shall be considered to have played out of turn with the penalty as in Rule 52.

56. a) If a player, in attempting to strike his own ball, touches (with his foot or mallet) another ball, his turn ends and both balls are replaced.

b) If after striking his ball (but before the conclusion of the stroke), the striker interferes with his ball there shall be no penalty (i.e., hitting one's own foot with ball in a hammer stroke). If it is at rest (or moving) it shall be placed where, as nearly as can be judged, it would otherwise come to rest. But after such interference, this ball cannot in that stroke make a roquet, score a point, or cause another ball to score a point or be displaced.

c) If a ball is interfered with by an outside agent, except weather, or accidentally by an opponent, in any way that materially affects the outcome of the stroke, that stroke shall be replayed. Otherwise, the ball shall be placed, as nearly as can be judged, where it would have come to rest, provided that no point or roquet can thereby be made. A rover ball prevented from scoring the peg by a pegged-out ball shall be placed where it would otherwise have come to rest.

57. a) A fault or misplay by a player must be called by his opponent before the next turn begins or else it will be automatically condoned.

b) If an out-of-turn fault is discovered by either side after two or more turns have been played (and condoned), play shall continue in the new sequence with all wicket points, deadness, or faults incurred during any turn up to that turn in which the fault is discovered being deemed valid.

58. If a player makes any stroke or strokes as the result of any false information concerning the state of the game supplied by his adversary, he shall have the right to replace and replay these strokes, providing that his claim is made before the end of the offending side's next turn. The deadness board represents an outside aid and, unless it is being inaccurately maintained by the opponent, may not be considered false information since the responsibility for remembering deadness or other aspects of the status of the game rests with the individual players.

PART 10. Referees

59. The role of the referee is to resolve disputes between players by reference to the book of rules. Any situation which does not appear to be covered by these rules shall be decided by the best judgment of the referee.

60. A referee should not intervene unless asked by the players. EXCEPTION: Rule 21 (re: clip placement or to call an official time out as in Rule 67 and 68b).

61. In the absence of an appointed referee, the players will act as their own joint referees, but there is an obligation on the adversary to watch the game, and if he fails to do so, the striker is, during such period, the sole referee. In doubles, all players share the rights and duties of a referee, and a reference to the striker includes his partner. (EXCEPTION: Rule 25 f.)

62. If, during a tournament match, a player fails to request that an adversary call a referee to observe a questionable stroke before it is taken, he may not appeal. Otherwise he may appeal as in Part 11.

PART 11. Tournament Play

63. For each tournament there shall be a tournament director selected who shall be empowered to: administrate, interpret and enforce the Rules of the Game; appoint a committee to assist and

provide referees, timekeepers and deadness board attendants; arrange the draw; assign handicaps; schedule matches; assign courts and otherwise direct all aspects of the competition, including the disposition of any appeal by players or teams not resolved by a referee.

64. In tournaments, a time limit either by stroke and/or per game may be set by a tournament committee before the start of the first tournament game. These time limits may be increased or decreased by the committee at the conclusion of each full round (e.g., first, quarter, or semi-final rounds as overall time and weather conditions dictate).

65. Until 15 minutes to the end of a time-limit game each player will be allowed no more than 60 seconds (45 in advanced game) to begin his stroke following the completion of the last stroke by either side. A stroke will be deemed completed when the ball comes to a complete stop or crosses the boundary line. The timekeeper will announce when 15 seconds remain in the time allotted for the next stroke and call "Time" when the 15 seconds has elapsed. Should the player not have struck his ball his turn ends and play resumes with the next player, after replacing balls displaced by the striker after time was called. During a match, each team is entitled to receive two (2) one-minute time-out periods (in addition to the 60 or 45 seconds allowed).

66. When fifteen minutes remain in the game, the timekeeper shall so announce, and thereafter each player will be allowed no more than 45 seconds to begin his turn. At one minute remaining the timekeeper shall turn his back on the court and will announce "Match Time" when the minute has elapsed.

67. a) When "Match Time" is called, the player in play shall complete his turn (which is his last), and each remaining ball shall have one turn in rotation. The side which has cumulatively passed through the greatest number of wickets, including the stake, is declared the winner, but if there is a tie, play shall continue in full rounds until the tie is broken or both balls of one side stake out.

b) When "Match Time" has been called and the player then playing has finished his turn, a one-minute official's time-out will be called to determine and announce the wicket score at that point. If a tie exists, the rotation remaining in the full round will be played. After that time-out, play shall resume under the 45-second-per-stroke limit until the tie is broken and the game has ended as in (a) above.

68. a) If, during the course of a tournament, either the players or the referee is unable to resolve a question of fact or law, they may appeal to the tournament director, who shall decide accordingly. If he by coincidence happens to have been a witness and is satisfied that he knows the answer, he should inform the players that he is deciding the subject matter of appeal by observation, and give his decision accordingly. If he is not so satisfied, he should decide the dispute by investigation. He should hear what the parties have to say. At his discretion he should hear witnesses. He should then give a decision to the best of his ability. If he is in doubt, he should, in the last resort, give a compromise decision, which may involve adjusting the clips arbitrarily and directing where the balls should be placed. This includes the right to decide that the players shall replay the disputed play or begin the game again.

b) A referee or tournament official may call for a time-out or stop play at any time during a match to adjudicate any dispute, delay or postpone completion of a match due to inclement weather or court conditions. The time taken by these official actions will be added to the time left in the match when play resumes.

ADVANCED RULES

WIRING

1. If at the end of a player's turn he has left the balls on the court arranged in such a way that the next opponent striker to play (whose ball is alive on 1, 2 or 3 other balls) is impeded from taking a direct stroke at any part of at least one ball upon which it is alive, that striker may lift his ball and place it in contact with any alive ball he chooses and take his croquet stroke.

A ball is said to be wired from another ball if: a) any part of an upright of a hoop or the peg would impede the direct course of any part of the striker's ball toward any part of the other ball; or

(b) any part of a hoop, peg or other ball upon which the striker is dead so interferes with any part of the swing of the mallet prior to impact between mallet and ball that the striker, with his usual style of play, cannot in order to make a roquet drive his ball freely towards any part of the other ball when striking the center of his ball with any part or face of his mallet: or if any part of the striker's ball is within the jaws of a wicket put there by the opponent. The mere interference of a hoop or the stake with the same stance of the striker does not constitute wiring.

2. If the next ball to play is dead on all three other balls, it may be left in any position on the court without being considered wired under this rule.

V.
The 9-Wicket Game

On the following pages are the rules for the 9-wicket, 2-stake croquet game as codified by the United States Croquet Association. Many of the rules are the same in both the 9-wicket and 6-wicket

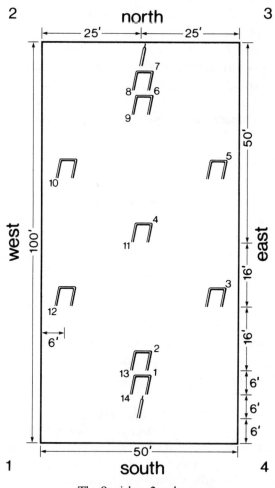

The 9-wicket, 2-stake court.

game. To avoid unnecessary duplication, when the rules are the same, we have not spelled out the 9-wicket rule but, rather, have referred you to the 6-wicket section. When the 9-wicket rule is different, we spell out the variation in full.

THE STANDARD COURT

The standard court is a rectangle, with the length two times the width (50 by 100 feet is recommended). Its boundaries shall be marked out clearly, the *inside* edge of the definitive border being the actual boundary. (Nylon string stapled or otherwise affixed to the ground can be used for boundary lines.) The court may be scaled down proportionately, but smaller than 30 by 60 feet is not recommended.

THE STANDARD SETTING

Two stakes shall be set at each end of the court, 6 feet from the adjacent end's boundary line, and equidistant from each side of the boundary line. The first and seventh wickets shall be 12 feet from the adjacent end line and equidistant from each sideline. The second and sixth wickets shall be 18 feet from the adjacent end line and equidistant from the two sidelines. The fourth wicket shall be set at the center of the court, equidistant from the side boundary lines. The far outside wickets (the third, fifth, tenth and twelfth) shall be set 34 feet from the adjacent end line and 6 feet from the adjacent boundary line. For smaller modified courts these dimensions may be reduced proportionately.

THE WICKETS

The wickets are the same as the 6-wicket game except they are all painted white.

THE STAKE, THE BALLS AND THE MALLETS

The stake, the balls and the mallets remain the same as in the 6-wicket game.

THE COURT ACCESSORIES

Are the same except clips are placed (as in Rule 21) on the top of the wicket for the first seven wickets and on the side for the last seven.

THE OBJECT OF THE GAME

SINGLES

The singles game is played between two players, of whom one plays the blue and black, the other the red and yellow balls. The object of the game is for a player to make both his balls score the 28 wicket points and 4 stake points, a total of 32 points, before his adversary.

DOUBLES

The doubles game is played between two sides, each side consisting of two players. One team plays the blue and black balls and the other the red and yellow balls. Each player plays only one ball throughout the game. As in singles, the object of the game is to have one team score the total of 32 points before its adversaries.

IN BOTH GAMES

A ball scores a wicket by passing through the wicket in the order and direction shown in the diagram on page 196. This is known as running a wicket. But a ball which has made a roquet cannot thereafter in the same stroke carom off that ball and score a point for itself. A ball which has scored all 14 wickets and the upper stake points is known as a rover. It can then score the stake point by hitting it.

HOW PLAY IS MADE

Play is made by striking a ball with a mallet. For the essentials of fair stroke, see Part 1 of the 6-Wicket Game. The player so playing is called the striker, and the ball that he strikes, the striker's ball. The striker may never strike an adversary's ball. By striking his own ball, the striker may cause any other ball to move and to score a point.

THE TURN

The players play each turn in sequence (Blue, Red, Black and Yellow). A player is initially entitled to one stroke in a turn, after which his turn ends, unless in that stroke his striker's ball has scored a wicket or stake point or hit another ball. When the wicket or upper stake is scored, the striker is entitled to play one continuation stroke. When another ball is hit, the striker is said to have made a roquet on that ball. He becomes dead on that ball and is entitled to two extra strokes. The first of these two strokes is known as the croquet stroke, and is made after moving and placing the striker's ball in contact with or up to one mallet head away from the roqueted ball, which, if in contact in the croquet stroke, is known as the croqueted ball. If in the croquet stroke the croqueted ball is sent off the court, or the striker's ball is sent off the court without first having made another roquet, the turn ends. During a turn the striker may roquet each ball he is alive on once, and he may make a further roquet on each ball provided that, since he has last roqueted it, his striker's ball has scored a wicket or upper stake point for itself and has thus cleared itself of its "deadness." Thus, by a series of strokes entitling him to continue, the striker may make one or more points, during one turn. Such a series is known as "making a break." But continuation strokes are not cumulative, so that a striker who:

a) scores a wicket or upper stake and hits another ball in the same stroke may take one continuation stroke or roquet the ball and take two;
b) makes a roquet in a croquet stroke, immediately takes croquet and continues accordingly;
c) scores a wicket or upper stake for his striker's ball in a croquet stroke, plays only one continuation stroke;
d) scores two wickets for his striker's ball in one stroke, plays only one continuation stroke.

BALL IN HAND, BALL OFF THE COURT AND REPLACEMENT OF BALLS OFF THE COURT AND NEAR BOUNDARIES

All are the same as in the 6-wicket game.

STRATEGY

Along with the basic objective of scoring 32 points first, each team or player (in singles) should employ those offensive or defensive moves that will restrict the progress of the opponents as in the 6-wicket game.

This version should be played as diagrammed, and the exceptions of the American 6-Wicket rules amended as noted.

PREFACE RULES

1. The Start: Each player must place his ball on a pre-designated spot between the first wicket and the lower stake (3 feet in front of the wicket). Upon striking a ball, the player is in the game and is considered "alive" on all other balls in the game. Play progresses in

rotation. Various clubs rule that a ball struck through the first or upper two wickets in one shot is entitled to two extra strokes. This is an optional local rule with the preferred rule being only one extra stroke for making both wickets.

2. Upper Stake Rule: The upper stake, when hit in proper order, rewards the player one extra stroke, removes any prior deadness and counts as one point (i.e., is treated as having made a wicket).

3. Rover Rule: Only when a rover ball is caused to strike the final stake by a partner or its player is that ball considered to have completed the game and is removed from the field (NOTE: partner must also stake-out for the team to win).

4. Should an opponent cause a rover ball to hit the final stake, the player so staked must remove his ball for his next two turns, and on his third turn (in rotation) must place his ball one mallet length or less from the final stake and hit up to the upper stake. In that shot, or subsequent turns, the player must hit the upper stake to return to the game as a rover (last deadness rule still stays in effect).

a) Only one rover may be staked out by the opponent at any one time. There is no limit to the number of times an opponent can stake out a rover ball.

b) A rover staked out by an opponent is not in the game until hitting the upper stake and shall be treated as if he did not exist (i.e., no one can play off him nor can he play off another) until hitting that upper stake, at which point he receives one extra stroke.

With the above as basic rule differences, the following are direct rule references to be used with the Standard American 6-Wicket Croquet Rules.

PART 1. Use of the Mallet
Rules 1 through 5 are consistent with those for the 6-wicket game.

PART 2. Starting the Game
6. Same as the 6-wicket game.

7. All balls must start from the starting tee one yard in front of the first wicket in the order shown on the stake (blue, red, black and yellow) and must continue in that order throughout the game, or until put out of play. Upon striking the ball, a player is in the game and is considered "alive" on all other balls in the game.

8 and 9. These rules do not apply in 9-wicket croquet.

10. Rule 10 is the same, except a player is alive on all balls that have played into the game but have not made this wicket.

11 to 13. These rules do not apply in 9-wicket croquet.

PART 3. Making a Wicket

Rules 14 through 20 are exactly the same.

21. The placement of clips is as in the 6-wicket game but with the clips placed on the crown for the first seven wickets and on one of the uprights for the final seven wickets.

PART 4. Wicket Points, Roquet, Croquet and Additional Strokes

22. Same as in the 6-wicket game except that in 9-wicket play, hitting the upper stake in proper order rewards the player one extra stroke, removes any prior deadness and counts as one point (i.e., is treated as having made a wicket).

23. Roquet: The same as in the 6-wicket game.

24. A player who makes his wicket, or hits the upper stake and hits a ball on the same play, must hit that ball again to receive two extra strokes from it. Unless he has driven either ball off the court in that same stroke, the striker may elect to take one continuation stroke and shall not be considered dead on the ball so hit. The hit ball is not replaced.

25. *The Croquet Stroke:* Optional rules for (A) Advanced (contact) or (B) Standard 9-wicket (mallet-head) play are described below, and the choice of which is to be followed should be agreed upon by all players prior to a game. See Special Note.*

A) *Advanced* (9-wicket croquet stroke): This is identical with 6-wicket Rule 25a through 25i in that the striker's ball must be placed in *contact* with the roqueted ball and must then cause that ball to move or shake during the first (croquet stroke) of the two strokes it has earned for having made the roquet shot.

B) *Standard* (9-wicket croquet stroke):
   a) The same as in 6-wicket croquet.
   b) After roqueting a ball upon which it is alive a player must either:
      1) bring his own ball to a mallet head or part thereof from the roqueted ball and play two strokes from there, but he

---

Special Note: The USCA urges all serious players to opt for the *contact* version of the rule above as it will surely improve all other 2-ball (croquet) strokes with practice and better prepare you for association level play anywhere in the world.

may not place his own ball through or under a wicket, or:

2) place his ball in contact with a roqueted ball and play a croquet stroke and then his second stroke, or:

3) place his ball against the one hit and hold it by foot or hand while driving the other away, and then play his second shot.

Under no circumstances may a player in taking any of the above shots place his ball out of bounds.

c) The same as in 6-wicket croquet.

d) and e) The same if played in contact.

f) Optional if playing contact.

g) The same as in 6-wicket croquet.

h) A foot or hand shot is optional for standard 9-wicket game but not recommended for the Advanced version.

i) The same as in 6-wicket croquet.

26. The same as in 6-wicket croquet.

PART 5. Bisques

27 to 32, concerning bisques and bisque use in handicap play, are the same for both the 6-wicket and the 9-wicket game.

PART 6. Dead Ball

33 to 36, concerning "deadness," are the same for both versions.

37. a) The same as in the 6-wicket game.

b) Optional rule for 9-wicket version provides relief of deadness for an opponent's ball when each ball hits the upper (or turning) stake (as occurs at the 1-back wicket in the 6-wicket game).

PART 7. Alive Ball

38 and 39 are the same in both versions of the game. The ball is considered alive when it is driven through a wicket or against the upper stake.

PART 8. Rover and Finishing the Game

40. A player who has made all the wickets and the upper stake in proper sequence becomes a rover and is considered alive on all other balls.

41. To clear or become alive from two- or three-ball deadness, a rover may go through any wicket in any direction or hit the upper stake, receiving an extra stroke. If the ball does not clear the wicket,

it must, unless knocked out, continue through in the same direction in order to be considered clean.

42. The same as in the 6-wicket game.

43. Only when a rover ball is caused to strike the final stake by a partner or its player is that ball considered to have completed the game and is removed from the field (NOTE: partner must also stake-out for the team to win). OPTIONAL RULE: Only a rover can stake out another rover (as in the 6-wicket rules).

44. Should an opponent cause a rover ball to hit the final stake, the player so staked must remove his ball for the next two turns and, on his third turn (in rotation), must place his ball one mallet length or less from the final stake and hit up to the upper stake. In that shot or subsequent turns, the player must hit the upper stake to return to the game as a rover (last deadness rule still stays in effect).

45. The same as in the 6-wicket game.

46 to 48. When one ball of a side has staked itself out (or been staked out by a rover partner ball), it is removed from the court immediately, and play continues in proper rotation with the staked-out ball losing all subsequent turns.

PART 9. Faults

49 to 52. The same as in the 6-wicket game.

53. (See optional Rule 25h above.) If playing a foot- or hand-shot version and the player's foot or hand loses contact with his ball, his turn ends and both balls remain where they lie.

54 to 58. The same as in the 6-wicket game.

PART 10. Referees

59 to 62. The rules dealing with referees and their duties are the same for both versions of croquet.

PART 11. Tournament Play

63 to 68. The rules for tournaments apply to both the 6- and 9-wicket games.

VI.
Rules of Golf Croquet

In the United States, as in the United Kingdom, golf croquet is played on a 6-wicket, 1-stake court layout as outlined below. It may, however, be played on a 9-wicket, 2-stake court by modifying the direction of play.

The rules relating to singles and doubles play apply subject to the following modifications:

1. **The Course**—a) Balls are played into the game from one mallet length from the center stake. In a short version, 7 points are contested: the first 6 and number 1 for the seventh point.

b) When 13 points are contested, the first 12 points are as in croquet. The thirteenth point is the third hoop. When 19 points are contested, the hoops 1-back to the rover are contested twice before contesting the third hoop. The peg is not contested.

2. **The Game**—a) All balls are always for the same hoop in order. The point is scored for the side whose ball first runs the hoop.

b) A short game is a contest for the best of 7 points, a middle length of 15 points and a long game for the best of 19 points. The game ends as soon as one side has scored a majority of the points to be played. It is customary to keep the tally of the score by declaring a side to be one or more points up or down or all square as the case may be.

c) Each turn consists of one stroke. The rules relating to roquet, croquet and continuation strokes do not apply.

d) The balls are played in the sequence blue, red, black, yellow. The opposing sides use blue and black and red and yellow.

3. **Running a Hoop**—If a striker causes one of the balls of his side partly to run a hoop (wicket) during a stroke, such a ball must begin afresh to run such a hoop before it can be scored by that ball in any subsequent stroke. But if an adversary causes a ball partly to run a hoop during a stroke, such a ball may run that hoop in a subsequent stroke. If a ball runs two hoops in one stroke, it scores both hoops for its side. The hoop point is scored by a ball that is cannoned, peeled or roqueted through a wicket except that a partner ball which has failed to clear the hoop on its own stroke may not be so driven through by his partner unless that ball was put into the wicket by an opponent.

4. **Jump Shot**—A player may not deliberately make his ball rise from the ground. If he does so accidentally or in ignorance of this law, and in consequence runs a hoop for his striker's or partner's ball, the point shall not be scored. Likewise, if in consequence thereof any ball is displaced, such a ball may be replaced at the option of the adversary side.

5. **Advancing a Ball Prematurely for the Next Point**—A player must play so as to contest the hoop in order rather than seek to gain an advantage for the next hoop in order. But a player bona-

fide contesting the hoop in order by, for example, attempting to cannon another ball, may legitimately play the stroke at the strength calculated to bring his ball to rest nearer the next hoop in order.

6. **Playing Out of Turn or with a Wrong Ball**—If the striker plays out of turn or with the wrong ball, that stroke and any subsequent strokes are null and void. All balls shall be replaced: the right ball shall be played by the correct player, and the other balls shall follow in due sequence. No points made during the period of error shall be scored. Any dispute should be settled by a referee.

7. **Methods of Handicapping**—Handicaps shall be allotted in the 13-point game according to Association Croquet handicaps as follows:

Regular Handicap	Golf Croquet Handicap
− 1 and under	0
− 1/2 to 2	1
2 1/2 to 6	2
6 1/2 to 9	3
10 to 12	4

In the shorter 7-point game the bisques received shall be decreased by 50 percent. In the longer game of 19 points the bisques received shall be increased by 50 percent. Notwithstanding the above provisions, special Golf Croquet handicaps may be given.

A Note on British and American Rules

Until the turn of the century all croquet-playing countries played the basic 4-ball game in a sequence of turns where blue would start, red would follow, then black and finally yellow would play; then the same rotation would be repeated until the game ended. England changed that law in 1920 in favor of the "either ball" or nonsequential game. This means that when it is the blue and black side's turn to play, either ball may be played no matter which had played during the player's turn. If a player wishes, he may continue to play the same ball each time it is his turn regardless of sequence.

The USCA rules retain the sequence rule.

Another key rule shared by all in 1900 was that involving the continuation of deadness by one ball on another. At that time, it was decided that a ball that was dead on another remained dead until that ball had made or cleared its next wicket in its proper order.

The British Association had changed this law by 1909, enabling all balls to be cleared of any deadness incurred previously at the start of each ball's next turn.

The USCA retains the rule that all deadness continues until the next wicket has been cleared.

Another differing rule has to do with roqueting (hitting) another ball off the court.

The English allow the striker to rush another ball out of bounds on his roquet stroke and continue to play after replacing that ball 36 inches into the court.

In the USCA rules, your turn ends if you knock another ball off the court on the roquet stroke. Both balls are brought in 9 inches—but you are not considered dead on that ball.

These three fundamental rules mark the primary difference in the British and U.S. Association games and call for strategies and tactics that, although we are at last playing on the same "pool table," are as different as 8-ball pool is from the rotation version of pool.

There are advantages and disadvantages to playing both games. On the surface, it would appear that the English game is easier and presumably faster. It gives you the freedom to hit balls off the court from any distance. It allows you not to be overly concerned about getting dead on other balls, because you will be clear on your next turn. And it gives you the choice of playing either of your side's balls at any time you choose.

In practice, however, English-rule games can and do run on for as many as five or six hours. Often it appears that the object of the game, that is, making wickets, has been forgotten altogether, as opponents jockey to pick up breaks and disdain shots at wickets unless they're only a foot away. The result is less than thrilling from the spectators' standpoint and may in fact be largely responsible for the relatively slow growth of the sport in England over the past twenty years.

In spite of our seemingly more complex needs to remember rotation and deadness, which compound the number of factors to be taken into consideration in planning tactics, the USCA game seems to race along. Because Americans *have* to make wickets to remove deadness, we shoot for them from dismaying distances. As a result, American games can and most often do end within an hour and a half, which is the time limit most often set in USCA tournament play. In fairness, the British Association rules tend to encourage better shot-making skills, owing to their forgiving nature.

In reporting on the 1982 US Challenge Cup matches in their official *Gazette*, South Africa's great champion Tom Barlow summed up his feelings on the relative merits of each game and its rules as follows:

"In retrospect it might be valuable to reflect on the advantages of the different games. The American game to my mind, does have certain advantages, the main one being that it is faster, less likely to be stereotyped and negative for minus players." He went on to say, "If in the future we are to play the Americans, I wonder if a mixed game cannot be worked out, and I suggest the following:

1. The American sequence and deadness system to be used, as this speeds the game up and adds tactical interest.
2. The (British) Association Boundary Laws (one yard in from the line) be applied as the American rules (9 inches) make it too difficult to pick up the fourth ball and reliable three-ball breaks are beyond most players (the USCA is considering an 18-inch inbounding rule).
3. The (British) Association Lift Laws* should be applied, "as this adds tactical interest and prevents the stymie."

He concluded by saying, "The laws of croquet have never been graven on tablets of stone, and it may be that with a bit of healthy cross-pollination, the (British) Association rules may change and the game flourish anew with hybrid vigor."

Understandably, a set of universally accepted rules would be most beneficial to the sport worldwide, but we see little likelihood of achieving this goal in the near future. Be it temperament or tempo, we Americans appear to favor the challenge of setting our own game in order with a marvelous spirit and gusto.

We look forward to seeing you on the courts.

---

*In the English game the opponent may "lift" one of its balls and shoot into the field from an area called a Baulk Line at each end of the court if that ball cannot clearly shoot at least one other ball on the court. This law prevents "wiring" or stymieing an opponent and will be introduced into the USCA Advanced rules in the near future.

APPENDICES

Glossary

alive—a word for a ball that has cleared a wicket, and thus is said to be "alive"—able to play—on all other balls.

all-around break—a player running all the wickets in a single turn.

approach shot—a shot designed to place the ball into position to clear its next wicket or to roquet another ball.

Aunt Emma—an overly cautious, uninspired and altogether dull player whose aim is to clear not many wickets but one wicket per turn.

ball-in-hand—a ball that, after hitting another ball or going out of bounds, must be picked up and moved.

bisque—a handicap consisting of an extra stroke given to weaker players in order to equalize the game. It allows a player to replay a shot from the spot where it was originally taken. The bisque is sometimes called a "take-over."

break—an unbroken series of wickets run by a single ball in combination with another ball (a two-ball break), two other balls (a three-ball break) or all the balls in play (a four-ball break).

break down—make an unsuccessful shot or commit a fault, thus causing a turn to end.

bye—a position on a tournament ladder where the player is without an opponent. He then advances to the next round without playing.

cannon shot—a combination shot, in which 1) a roquet is made on the same stroke as the croquet stroke, or 2) the croqueted ball is driven into a third ball to displace it.

clearing (or cleaning)—becoming "undead" by running a wicket, or being relieved of deadness under the rules.

clips—markers made in the same colors as the balls which are placed on wickets to indicate which wickets the balls are going for next and in which direction on the court they are going.

condoning—failure of a player to claim a foul within the limit of claims.

contact—a move in which, after a roquet shot, the player places his ball in contact with the ball he has just roqueted and prepares to take croquet.

continuation shot—an extra shot, earned by clearing a wicket. Also, the shot taken after the croquet stroke.

corner—make a defensively shrewd shot into a corner.

Croquet Association, The—the British governing body founded as the All England Croquet Club.

croquet stroke (or shot)—the stroke in which, after a player roquets another ball, he places his ball next to the roqueted ball and, by striking his ball, moves both balls.

cross wire (or Peg)—a leave in which the opponent's balls are left on each side of a wicket or peg, thus preventing them from hitting each other.

crush shot—an illegal shot used to knock a ball through a wicket so that during the stroke the mallet, ball and upright are all in contact at the same time.

cut rush—a single-ball shot that is played so that the roqueted ball (the "rushed" ball) goes off at a desired angle.

deadness—describing a player who has roqueted another ball. He is said to be "dead" on that ball—that is, he cannot play off that ball again—until his ball clears its next wicket.

deadness board—a board placed on the sidelines to aid the players and spectators in keeping track of which balls are "dead" on other balls.

double banking—playing two separate games on the same court at the same time with two sets of different-colored balls.

double elimination—a type of tournament in which a player must lose two matches in order to be eliminated.

double tap—a fault in which the striker's ball is accidentally hit twice in one stroke.

double target—two balls placed close together so that the target area is, in effect, doubled.

drive shot—a shot made by hitting squarely on the ball during the croquet stroke, causing the forward ball to go about three times farther than the striker's.

fault—an unacceptable stroke, or an action resulting in a penalty.

flags—visual aids to mark the corners of the croquet court.

foot shot—a croquet shot taken with the striker's foot on the ball, legal only in backyard croquet.

forestalling—claiming a misplay when a player observes that an opponent has committed or is about to commit a fault and stops him before his next stroke.

four-ball break—the mainstay of successful croquet, a break that uses all four balls to make a number of wickets, ideally allowing the striker to take his ball all the way around the court.

half-bisque—an extra shot used in handicap doubles and in some singles games, allowing the striker to re-take a shot but not allowing him to clear the wicket and score a point with the take-over shot.

hoop—used interchangeably with "wicket."

hoop-bound—describing a stroke or swing that is impeded by the wicket.

is for—the next wicket a ball must clear, as in "red 'is for' the second wicket."

jaws—entrance to the uprights of a wicket.

join up—play a ball to a spot near its partner ball.

jump shot—a shot in which the ball is struck so that it leaves the ground, thus avoiding an obstructing ball, wicket or stake.

laying a break—positioning balls at future wickets so that they can be used to set up breaks.

leave—the position on the court where a player leaves his and the opponents' balls at the end of his turn.

limit of claims—the time during which a fault may be called.

out of bounds—describing a ball whose vertical axis has crossed the boundary line.

pass—to waive or pass up a turn.

pass roll—a croquet stroke that sends the striker's ball farther than the croqueted ball.

peel—to cause a ball other than one's own to make its next wicket.

peg—the center stake.

peg-out—the final shot of a game, when a ball scores the peg or stake point.

penultimate—the next-to-last wicket.

pioneer ball—in a three-ball or four-ball break, the ball that is sent ahead to the wicket that is one beyond the wicket you are going for.

pivot ball—the middle ball in a four-ball break usually left in the middle of the court.

pull—in the croquet shot, the tendency for a ball to curve in from its line of aim.

push—keeping the mallet head on the ball after hitting it, allowable only on the croquet shot, and then only if the mallet doesn't speed up after making contact.

questionable stroke—a play of doubtful legality, or one that has a large possibility of leading to a foul. When the striker anticipates such a play, he should call for the referee to observe the shot before he attempts it.

roll shots—a croquet shot in which both balls travel along the same line. Variations include the half-roll, the three-quarter roll and full and pass rolls.

roquet—a shot in which the striker's ball hits another upon which it is alive. It is followed by a croquet shot and then a continuation stroke.

rover—a player whose ball has made the last wicket, or a ball that has cleared the final wicket but has not yet hit the peg.

running a wicket—hitting a ball through a wicket so that a mallet head run down the approach side of the wicket does not touch the ball.

rush—a roquet that sends the roqueted ball to a predetermined position.

rush line—a line extending between the ball about to be rushed and its intended target spot. A player imagines the rush line to assist him in determining a rush stroke.

scratch player—as in golf, a player who receives no handicap (bisque).

sight line—a line usually set lengthwise on top of the mallet head to aid the player in aiming the direction of his stroke.

smasher—a wooden hammer used to drive wickets into the ground.

split shot—a croquet shot that sends the two balls at divergent angles.

stalk—to stand behind the ball and walk toward it in order to be sure it is properly aimed.

sticky wicket—a particularly tight wicket that is difficult to clear without getting stuck in its jaws.

stop-shot—a croquet shot that sends the croqueted ball much farther than the striker's ball.

striker—the player whose turn it is to play.

stroke—a movement of the mallet in the process of striking a ball, whether the ball is successfully struck or not.

stymie—a ball blocking the intended path of the striker's ball when the striker's ball is dead on it.

take-off shot—a croquet stroke in which the croqueted ball moves very little and the striker's ball moves a greater distance.

take-over—see "bisque."

tice—a shot that places the striker's ball in a position where the opponent is tempted (or enticed) to shoot at it and miss (from "entice").

Time limit—in USCA tournament play, usually 1½ to 2 hours, but may vary depending on the number of courts and entrants.

waive—to pass up a turn. The ball is then considered to have been placed where it lies.

wicket—a straight- or curved-topped arch, usually made of iron, through which a ball must be driven (synonymous with "hoop" in England).

winter wickets—bent iron wickets often used when the ground is hard or frozen.

wired ball—a ball behind a wicket or peg which can't be hit by the striker's ball because of the obstruction.

The United States Croquet
Hall of Fame

Each year the trustees of the Croquet Foundation of America consider individual nominees whose contributions to the growth and enjoyment of the game of croquet in the United States would merit their induction in the United States Croquet Hall of Fame. Since 1979, its inaugural year, the following distinguished American croquet players have been elected:

George Abbott
Paul Butler
Margaret Emerson
Raoul Fleischmann
Andrew Fuller
Samuel Goldwyn
John David Griffin
William Harbach
W. Averell Harriman
Moss Hart
Howard Hawks
William Hawks
Milton "Doc" Holden
Louis Jourdan
George S. Kaufman
John Lavalle
Mrs. Carvel (Susie) Linden
Duncan McMartin

Harpo Marx
Jean Negulesco
Jack Osborn
Mrs. Ogden (Lilian) Phipps
Edmund A. Prentis III
Richard Rodgers
Mrs. Richard (Dorothy) Rodgers
Michael Romanoff
George Sanders
Frederick Schock, Jr.
Herbert Bayard Swope, Jr.
Herbert Bayard Swope, Sr.
S. Joseph Tankoos
Francis O. Tayloe
Alexander Woollcott
Gig Young
John and Melga Young
Darryl F. Zanuck

USCA National Champions

SINGLES

Year	Winners	Runners-Up
1977	J. Archie Peck, Palm Beach	Jack Osborn, New York
1978	Richard Pearman, Bermuda	Jack Osborn, New York
1979	J. Archie Peck, Palm Beach	Richard Pearman, Bermuda
1980	J. Archie Peck, Palm Beach	Arthur Bohner, Westhampton, N.Y.
1981	Richard Pearman, Bermuda	Jack Osborn, New York
1982	J. Archie Peck, Palm Beach	Richard Pearman, Bermuda

DOUBLES

Year	Winners	Runners-Up
1977	Jack Osborn & J. Archie Peck	Nelga & John Young, Bermuda
1978	E. A. (Ted) Prentis & Arthur Bohner	Jack Osborn & J. Archie Peck
1979	Jack Osborn & J. Archie Peck	E. A. Ted Prentis & Arthur Bohner
1980	Ted & Ned Prentis	Richard Pearman & John Young
1981	Ted & Ned Prentis	Richard Pearman & John Young
1982	Archie & Mark Burchfield (Kentucky)	Jack Osborn & J. Archie Peck

USCA NATIONAL CLUB TEAM CHAMPIONSHIPS

Year	Club/Winners	Club/Runners-Up
1980	New York Croquet Club Jack Osborn & Ted Prentis	Westhampton Mallet Club Alfred Heath & Ned Prentis
1981	New York Croquet Club Jack Osborn & Ted Prentis	Aulander Croquet Club, No. Carolina Francis O. Tayloe & Mack Penwell
1982	New York Croquet Club Jack Osborn & Ted Prentis	Arizona Croquet Club Stanley Patmor & James Bast

USCA National Intercollegiate Champions
Singles

Year	Winners	Runners-Up
1982	Vassar College John C. Osborn	University of Florida G. Briggs Kilborne

Doubles

Year	Winners	Runners-Up
1982	University of Florida G. Briggs Kilborne & Michael Fuller	Yale University Kevin Lewis & Garry Wills

1982 USCA National Ratings

The following USCA ratings are based on the final standings of all individual competitors entered in these major Class "A" 1982 USCA Championship tournaments:

> USCA National Singles Championships—New York, N.Y.
> USCA National Doubles Championships—New York, N.Y.
> USCA National Club Team Championships—Palm Beach, Fla.

Annually hereafter, all USCA–sanctioned regional, sectional, district and club championship tournaments will be computed into the comprehensive overall rankings for all individuals entering these events.

1982 USCA SINGLES STANDINGS

USCA Player	Home State
1. J. Archie Peck	Florida
2. Richard Pearman	Bermuda
3. John Young	Bermuda
4. Ted Prentis	New York
5. Paul Kemmerly	Arizona
Nelga Young	Bermuda
7. Archie Burchfield	Kentucky
James Dushek	Illinois
9. Arthur Bohner	New York
William Hiltz	New York
Jack Osborn	New York
Mack Penwell	No. Carolina
13. Jim Bast	Arizona
Jim Hermann	Arizona
Xandra Kayden	Massachusetts
John C. Osborn	New York
17. Don Degnan	New York
Richard Dougherty	New York
Barry Fitzpatrick	California
Mike Hart	Illinois
Peter Hull	Connecticut
Kiley Jones	New York
Robert Kroeger	Massachusetts
Ned Prentis	N.Y./Florida
25. Sanford Brown	Connecticut
David Caulkins	Connecticut
Tom Hunt	Pennsylvania
Richard Illingworth	New York
Ellery McClatchy	New York
Ben Smith	Massachusetts
Doug White	No. Carolina
Cortland Wood	N.Y./Florida

(Based on the final standings in the National Singles Championships. Ties are listed in alphabetical order.)

1982 USCA DOUBLES GRAND PRIX STANDINGS

USCA Player	Home State
1. Jack Osborn*	New York
2. Archie Peck*	Florida
3. Richard Pearman*	Bermuda
4. Jim Bast*	Arizona
5. Archie Burchfield*	Kentucky
Ted Prentis*	New York
7. Mark Burchfield	Kentucky
Kiley Jones*	New York
John Young*	Bermuda
10. Stanley Patmor*	Arizona
11. Richard Illingworth	New York
12. Paul Kemmerly	Arizona
Dan Mahoney	Florida
John C. Osborn	New York
Ned Prentis*	N.Y./Florida
Cortland Wood*	N.Y./Florida
17. Xandra Kayden*	Massachusetts
Mack Penwell	No. Carolina
Doug White	No. Carolina
20. Robert Clayton	New York
Richard Dougherty	New York
Dana Dribben*	Florida
Josie Finsness	Bermuda
Hal Finsness	Bermuda
William Hiltz	New York
Robert Kroeger	Massachusetts
Herbert Swope	Florida
Nelga Young*	Bermuda
29. Sanford Brown	Connecticut
David Caulkins	Connecticut
Don Degnan	New York
Barry Fitzpatrick	California
Jacqui Fitzpatrick	California
Alfred Heath	Florida
Jim Hermann	Arizona
Jay Rossbach	New York
Cathy Tankoos	New York

38. Art Bohner   New York
    James Dushek   Illinois
    Mike Hart   Illinois
    Jack Hight   Florida
    David Hull   Connecticut
    Peter Hull   Connecticut
    Thomas Hunt   New Jersey
    Walter Janitz   Indiana
    Ellery McClatchy   New York
    Jack McMillin   Florida
    Walter Margulies   N.Y./Fla.
    Ed Montague   New York
    Jeffrey Nack   Illinois
    Fred Supper   Conn./Fla.
    Henry White   New York
    Dudley Woodbridge   New Jersey
54. Peyton Ballenger   No. Carolina
    Christopher Bergen   Massachusetts
    Stan Bilek   New Jersey
    Rudulph Carter   N.Y./R.I.
    Norman Cook   Connecticut
    Nick Etcheverry   Massachusetts
    Stuart Gregory   New York
    John Hunter   Connecticut
    Merlin Karlock   Illinois
    Alex Kloubek   New Jersey
    Catherine Nack   Illinois
    George Ripley   Massachusetts
    Eugene Schnell   N.Y./Mass.
    John Schott   Massachusetts
    Johnathan Sweet   New York
    Bobby Wilhoite   Kentucky

(Based on final standings in the National Doubles and/or the National Club Team Championships. An * denotes those competing in both events with the remaining competing in one event or the other. Ties are listed in alphabetical order.)

1982 USCA NATIONAL COLLEGIATE STANDINGS

1. G. Briggs Kilborne (U. of Florida)
2. John C. Osborn (Vassar)
3. M. Kent Karlock (Harvard)
4. Ron Fisher (Brandeis)
    Michael Fuller (U. of Florida)
6. Kevin Lewis (Yale)
    Garry Wills (Yale)
8. Robin Urban (Yale)
9. Burns Patterson (Vassar)
10. John Sweet (Columbia)
11. Brad Farkas (Harvard)
12. Richard Thomas (U.S.C.)
13. Stuart Gregory (Columbia)
14. Dan Mahoney (Vassar)
    Peter Zahos (Yale)
16. Frank Russell (Vassar)
17. Alex Hittle (Brown)

    Rick Weinstein (Brown)
19. John Adelman (Columbia)
20. Lisa Sanchez-Corea (U.S.C.)
    David Silverstein (Brandeis)
    Jeff Wallach (Vassar)
23. Matt Salinger (Princeton)
    Thor Thors (Princeton)
25. Mark Bilski (Vassar)
    Arthur Bingham (Columbia)
    Gordon Bloom (Harvard)
    Peter Kelley (Harvard)
    Chris Langhoff (Vassar)
30. Vance Brown (Brown)
    Elaine Donaldson (Barnard)
    Rob Hawkins (Brown)
    Laura Sacher (Barnard)
34. Demetrios Diakolios (Vassar)

The USCA Collegiate Division ratings are based on the final standings of the individual competitors entered in the following 1982 USCA Collegiate Championship Events:

> National Intercollegiate Croquet Championships
> Singles and Doubles—Palm Beach, Fla.
> Eastern Regional Collegiate Croquet Championships
> Doubles only—New York, N.Y.

Collegiate ratings are currently not factored into the overall USCA ratings, as they will be in future Grand Prix computations.

United States Croquet Association Member Clubs (as of February 1983)

ALASKA
> Alaska Croquet Club, Anchorage

ARIZONA
> Arizona Biltmore Hotel, Phoenix
> Arizona Croquet Club, Phoenix
> Black Trail Croquet Club, Phoenix
> Scottsdale House Croquet Club, Scottsdale

CALIFORNIA
Beverly Hills Croquet Club, Beverly Hills
Cabernet Croquet Club, Santa Rosa
La Jolla Croquet Club, La Jolla
Los Angeles Croquet Club, Encino
Luby Croquet & Racquet Club, Newport Beach
Rancho Santa Fe Croquet Club, Rancho Santa Fe
San Francisco Croquet Club, San Francisco
San Mateo Croquet Club, San Mateo
Santa Rosa Croquet Club, Santa Rosa
Sunnyside Croquet Club, Tahoe City
University of Southern California Croquet Club, Los Angeles

COLORADO
Park Hill Croquet Club, Denver
Vail Croquet Club, Vail

CONNECTICUT
Minerva Place Croquet Club, Old Greenwich
Round Island Mallet Club, Greenwich
Yale Croquet Team, New Haven

FLORIDA
The Beach Club, Palm Beach
The Everglades Club, Palm Beach
Gasparilla Mallet Club, Boca Grande
Palm Beach Croquet Club, Palm Beach
Palm Beach Polo & Country Club, West Palm Beach
Sandpiper Bay Croquet Club, Port St. Lucie
University of Florida Croquet Club, Gainesville
Vanderbilt Gulfside Croquet Club, Naples

GEORGIA
Argonne Drive Croquet Club, Atlanta
Georgia Croquet Club, Williamson

HAWAII
Oahu Croquet Club, Honolulu
Wailea Croquet Club, Kihei, Maui

ILLINOIS
Bon Vivant Country Club, Bourbonnais
Chicago Croquet Club
The Meadow Club (Chicago), Rolling Meadow

INDIANA
Sound Bend Croquet Club, Mishawaka

KENTUCKY
Stamping Ground Croquet Club, Stamping Ground

MAINE
Claremont Croquet Club, Southwest Harbor

MASSACHUSETTS
Berkshire Mallet Club, Sandisfield
Blantyre Croquet Club, Lenox
Boston Croquet Club, Boston
Brandeis Croquet Club, Waltham
Edgartown Mallet Club, Edgartown
Harvard Croquet Club, Cambridge
Marion Mallet Club, Marion
Mount Holyoke Croquet Club, Mt. Holyoke
Oyster Harbors Croquet Club, Osterville
Pheasant Hill Croquet Club, South Hamilton
Richmond Mallet Club, Pittsfield
Smith College Croquet Club, Northampton
Smith's Point Croquet Club, Great Island
Tyringham Mallet Club, Tyringham
Wellesley College Croquet Club, Wellesley

MICHIGAN
Grosse Point Croquet Club, Grosse Point
Harbor Balls & Mallet Club, Harbor Point

MINNESOTA
Minnetonka Mallet Club, Wayzata

MISSISSIPPI
Gulf Coast Croquet Club, Bay St. Louis

NEW HAMPSHIRE
Freedom Mallet Club, Freedom
Hampstead Croquet Club, Hampstead
Strawberry Banke Museum Croquet Club, Portsmouth

NEW JERSEY
Bohemia Croquet Club, Roseland
Fox Chase Croquet Club, Gladstone

Green Gables Croquet Club, Spring Lake
Princeton Croquet Club, Princeton
Short Hills Croquet Club, Short Hills

NEW YORK
Barnard Croquet Club, New York City
Boss Street Croquet Club, Bolivar
Chipmunk Hollow Croquet Club, Franklin
Columbia Croquet Club, New York City
Croquet Club of Rochester, Rochester
East Hampton Croquet Club, East Hampton
Locusts Croquet Club, Staatsburg
The Meadow Club of Southampton, Southampton
Millerton Croquet Club, Millerton
New York Croquet Club, New York City
Partidge Hill Croquet Club, Carmel
Plumfields Croquet Club, Southampton
Quantuck Bay Croquet Group, Quioque
Tuxedo Park Croquet Club, Tuxedo Park
Vassar Croquet Club, Poughkeepsie
Westhampton Mallet Club, Westhampton Beach
Westhampton Tennis & Sports Club, Westhampton Beach
Woodstock Croquet Club, Woodstock

NORTH CAROLINA
Aulander Croquet Club, Aulander
Grandfather Golf and Country Club, Linville
Pinehurst Hotel & Country Club, Pinehurst
Pine Mallet Club, Southern Pines
Salisbury Croquet Club, Salisbury

OKLAHOMA
Colonies Balls & Mallet Club, Oklahoma City

OREGON
Western Oregon Croquet Association, Creswell

PENNSYLVANIA
Bucks County Mallet Club, New Hope

RHODE ISLAND
Brown University Croquet Club, Providence
Newport Croquet Club, Newport

SOUTH CAROLINA
  Hilton Head Croquet Club, Hilton Head

TENNESSEE
  Knoxville Croquet Club, Knoxville

TEXAS
  Aerie Croquet Club, Amarillo
  Austin Mallet Club, Austin
  Villa Saralita Croquet Club, Dallas

VIRGINIA
  Modern Lawn Sport Club, Blacksburg
  Sandy Fields Croquet Club, Richmond
  University of Virginia Croquet Club, Charlottesville

VIRGIN ISLANDS
  Bombay Mallet & Wicket Croquet Club, Christiansted, St. Croix

WASHINGTON
  Chirp Chirp Mallet Club, Pullman
  Puget Sound Croquet Club, Seattle
  Seattle Croquet Club, Seattle

WASHINGTON, D.C.
  Catholic University Croquet Club

International Division

BERMUDA
  The Croquet Club of Bermuda, Hamilton

COSTA RICA
  Costa Rica Croquet Club, San Jose

JAMAICA
  Jamaica Inn Croquet Club, Ochos Rios

MEXICO
   Cuernavaca Croquet Club, Cuernavaca, Morelos
   San Miguel Allende Croquet Club, San Miguel Allende

For addresses and telephone numbers of these clubs, write or call the United States Croquet Association, 635 Madison Avenue, New York, New York 10022, (212) 688-5495.

USCA Informational Offerings

PUBLICATIONS

The United States Croquet Association publishes the Official Rules for American 6-Wicket and 9-Wicket Croquet as well as Golf Croquet. Literally pocket-sized (4 × 6 inches), the rule book is invaluable for ending disputes on the greensward. The cost of the Rule Book is $2.50 including postage.

The Association also publishes, each spring and fall, the *U.S. Croquet Gazette*. This semi-annual newsmagazine reprints the best of the year's mass-media articles about croquet and keeps its readers up to date about new clubs, tournament schedules and results. Back copies are available from the USCA; the fall 1979 *Gazette* costs $3; the fall 1980, 1981 and 1982 issues cost $2.50 each. Postage is included.

To order these publications, or to request a catalogue of USCA informational offerings, write the United States Croquet Association, 635 Madison Avenue, New York, New York 10022, or call (212) 688-5495.

VIDEOTAPES

In 1981 the Croquet Foundation of America produced a 40-minute videotape that dovetails neatly with this book. Starting with a tour of the court, *Croquet: A Primer* shows top players demonstrating the various grips, stances, swings and shots. Because it was filmed at the USA vs. England matches, it features English greats John Solomon, Bernard Neal and Nigel Aspinall executing two-ball, three-ball and four-ball breaks. As a visual teaching aid, this tape is without peer. It is available in ½-inch videotape cassettes in either the VHS or Beta II formats at a cost of $50 plus $2.50 postage and handling.

Also available is a 10-minute videotape titled *America's Most Misunderstood Sport*, which serves as an entertaining introduction to the USCA game and its various competitive and social attractions. It is available in either the VHS or Beta II formats for $25 plus $2.50 postage and handling, or it can be ordered in combination with *Croquet: A Primer* for $60 plus $2.50 postage and handling.

Additional instructional tapes are produced on an ongoing basis. For a listing of new tapes, or to order those named above, contact the United States Croquet Association, 635 Madison Avenue, New York, New York 10022 (phone: 212-688-5495).

Equipment

A number of American manufacturers have begun to make association croquet equipment. For information about these manufacturers and a list of retailers who will be carrying their equipment, contact the United States Croquet Association.

Croquet International, Ltd., is the official United States agent for association croquet equipment manufactured by Jaques of London. In addition to selling complete sets, Croquet International also sells mallets, balls, wickets, pegs, clips, flags and other accessories. For a catalogue, price information and a list of retailers carrying Jaques equipment, contact Croquet International at 635 Madison Avenue, New York, New York 10022 (phone: 212-688-5495).

Photo and Drawing Credits

Page 25, 26, 27 top: Richard Carver Wood; 27 bottom: Jean Negulesco; 41: United States Croquet Association; 42: unknown; 44, 45: Cliff Johnson, 50: Croquet International, Ltd.; 54, 55: William Powers; 57: Croquet International, Ltd.; 58, 60, 61, 63, 69: William Powers; 71: United Press International; 73, 75, 76, 77, 78, 79, 81, 83, 85: William Powers; 87: Alan Scheuch; 89, 91: William Powers; 95, 96: Alan Scheuch; 99, 100-101, 104: William Powers; 106-7: Alan Scheuch; 108-9, 110-11, 112-13, 114-15: William Powers; 171: United States Croquet Association.